Government and Society in Nineteenth-Century Britain
Commentaries on British Parliamentary Papers

POPULATION AND EMIGRATION

By the same authors:

P. FORD

The Economics of Collective Bargaining (Blackwell, Oxford, 1958)
Social Theory and Social Practice (Irish University Press, 1968)

P. & G. FORD

Hansard's Catalogue and Breviate of Parliamentary Papers, 1696-1834 (IUP 1000-volume series, General Indexes, Volume 1)
Select List of British Parliamentary Papers, 1833-99 (Irish University Press, 1969)
A Breviate of Parliamentary Papers, 1900-16 (Irish University Press, 1969)
A Breviate of Parliamentary Papers, 1917-39 (Irish University Press, 1969)
A Breviate of Parliamentary Papers, 1940-54 (Blackwell, Oxford, 1961)
Luke Graves Hansard's Diary, 1814-41 (Blackwell, Oxford, 1962)

P. & G. FORD AND DIANA MARSHALLSEY

Select List of British Parliamentary Papers, 1955-64 (Irish University Press, 1970)

D. V. GLASS

Population Policies and Movements in Europe (Clarendon Press, Oxford, 1940)
The Trend and Pattern of Fertility in Great Britain (H.M.S.O., 1954, with E. Grebenik)
Social Mobility in Britain, editor and contributor (Routledge and Kegan Paul, London, 1954)
Introduction to Malthus, editor and contributor (Watts, London, 1953)
Population in History, co-editor and contributor (Edward Arnold, London, 1965)
Population and Social Change, co-editor and contributor (Edward Arnold, London, 1972)
Numbering the People (Saxon House, 1973)

P. A. M. TAYLOR

The Industrial Revolution in Britain, editor (D. C. Heath, 1958, rev. 1970)
The English Civil War, editor (D. C. Heath, 1960)
Expectations Westward: The Mormons and the Emigration of their British Converts in the 19th Century (Oliver and Boyd, 1965)
The Distant Magnet: European Emigration to the United States (Eyre and Spottiswood, 1971)

Government and Society in Nineteenth-Century Britain
Commentaries on British Parliamentary Papers

POPULATION
AND
EMIGRATION

D. V. Glass

P. A. M. Taylor

Introduction by P. and G. Ford

IRISH UNIVERSITY PRESS

Irish University Press British Parliamentary Paper Series
CHIEF EDITORIAL ADVISERS
P. Ford
Professor Emeritus, Southampton University
Mrs G. Ford

ISBN 0 7165 2219 5 (case bound) 0 7165 2220 9 (paper bound)
Library of Congress Catalogue Card Number 73-92944

All forms of micro-publishing
© Irish Academic Press Ltd.

Published by IRISH ACADEMIC PRESS LTD
46 Kildare Street, Dublin 2, Ireland

Printed in Great Britain by
The Whitefriars Press Ltd., London and Tonbridge

Contents

Abbreviations

C., Cd., Cmd.	Command Paper	mins. of ev.	minutes of evidence
Ch.	Chairman	q. (qq.)	question(s)
ev.	evidence	R. Com.	Royal Commission
HC	House of Commons	Rep.	Report
HL	House of Lords	Sel. Cttee.	Select Committee

Citations

The form used for House and Command papers is:

> session/paper no./volume no./volume page no.

Example:

> 1845(602)xii,331

If the title has not been given in the text, the form should be preceded by the title and description:

> title and description/session/paper no./volume no./volume page no.

Examples:

> Game Law. Sel. Cttee. Rep.; 1845(602)xii,331
> London Squares. R.Com. Rep.; 1928-29 Cmd. 3196,viii,111

References are to the *House of Commons* bound sets, *except* where the paper is in the House of Lords set only. From this it follows:

a. Where the paper is the report of a Lords select committee (communicated to the Commons) it must be marked HL to indicate this and to distinguish it from a Commons select committee:
Example:

> Sale of Beer. Sel.Cttee.HL.Rep.; 1850(398)xviii,438.

b. Where the paper is in the Lords papers only, HL should be added to the paper number. This can be done in the form HL(259) or (HL.259).

c. For a reference to a statement on a particular page of a paper, the title and description should be followed by the *printed* page number of the paper:

> title etc./printed page no./session/paper no./volume no./vol. page no.

Example:

> Finance and Industry. Cttee.Rep.p.134;1930-31Cmd.3897,xiii,219

Where the reference is to the Irish University Press the citation is:

> IUP/subject/title/volume no.

Example:

> IUP Monetary Policy: General 4.

Introduction to Parliamentary Papers

P. and G. Ford

A fully comprehensive definition of parliamentary papers would include all those which form part of the necessary machinery of parliamentary government, even those concerned with the procedures of the day-to-day business. But from the point of view of the researcher three groups are of primary importance. The first group, the Journals, record the things done in parliament. The second group, the Debates, record the things said in parliament (the publication of the House of Commons Debates became known as Hansard throughout the world and was at first not an official but a private venture receiving public subsidy). The third group, Papers arising in or presented to parliament deal with the formulation, development and execution of its policy. It is to this third group, for many years known as 'Blue Books' because of the blue paper with which most of them were covered, that the name Parliamentary Papers became particularly attached.

After 1801 the papers were gathered together and bound in two separate sessional sets, one for the House of Commons and the other for the House of Lords. These volumes include reports of select committees, composed of a limited number of members of either House appointed to examine particular problems, and reports of royal commissions and committees of enquiry appointed in form by the Crown though on the advice of ministers or by ministers themselves. These latter have the double advantage of comprising persons from outside the House thought to be experts on the subjects in hand, persons prominent in public affairs or representative of some body of opinion, experience or interest, and of not being limited in their work to the length of a parliamentary session. All these bodies reported the results of their enquiries together with the evidence taken to the authority which appointed them. The reports of select committees and the papers which departments were required by Act to send to parliament, because they originated *in* the House were grouped into a numbered series as House Papers. Royal commissions reported formally to the Crown — even submitting massive volumes of evidence for it to read — and committees reported to the minister concerned. Because these were the work of bodies *outside* the House, the papers were brought to the House and incorporated in the Sessional Papers through the use of an historic formula which embodies much of the development of constitutional monarchy, 'Presented by Command'.

It was these committees and commissions which uncovered the evils of the work of children in factories and mines, the evils of bad housing and sanitation and of inadequate water supply in the new sprawling towns created by the Industrial Revolution, as well as the difficulties relating to monetary policy and the new phenomenon of recurrent trade depressions. The witnesses brought before the enquiring bodies included the victims of the new industrial conditions – little children who had worked in factories and mines, the exploited immigrants in the sweated trades, and the leaders of the early efforts to unionize workmen, such as John Gast in 1815, John Doherty in 1838 and the whole of the top leadership of the great trade unions in 1867-69. What is more remarkable is that the oral evidence was printed verbatim. Even Marx was impressed by the commissions' plenary powers for getting at the truth, the competence and feedom from partisanship and respect of persons displayed by the English Factory Inspectors, the Medical Officers reporting on public health and the Commissioners of Enquiry into the exploitation of women and children, into housing and food. There is no parallel in the world for such a series of searching and detailed enquiries covering so long a span of years and embracing every phase of the transition from a rural aristocratic society to an industrialized democracy. It is the most significant of these reports on a century of investigation, the 'policy papers', that are embodied in the Irish University Press series.

The method of personal examination of witnesses had occasionally to be modified when central hearings were not practicable. Before the Benthamite conception of a unified central and local government machine had been realized in practice, the central authorities often knew little of what was going on in the localities. The many thousands of parishes administered the poor laws in their own ways so that the *Royal Commission on the Poor Laws* (1834) had to send round assistant commissioners to carry out and report on a detailed standardized plan of enquiry. The *Royal Commission on Municipal Corporations* (1835) had to make district enquiries on how the boroughs and 'places claiming to be boroughs' conducted their affairs. The effect of adverse forces on agriculture could be country-wide: the *Royal Commission on the Depressed Condition of the Agricultural Interests* (1881-82), on *Agricultural Depression* (1894-97) and the *Labour Commission* (1892-94) looking into agricultural labour, each made use of assistant commissioners to find out what was common and what was different in the problems of the various districts. These papers are a mine of information.

There are also the various famous reports by great civil servants, such as Horner's on the enforcement of factory legislation, Tremenheere's on the state of the mining districts, bound in the sets under the heading of commissioners' reports, and Southwood Smith's on the *Physical Causes of*

Sickness and Mortality to which the Poor are Exposed, tucked away in an appendix to an annual report.

Two aspects of these investigations — the membership of the committees and the importance of British constitutional procedure — are worthy of note. The fullness and considerable integrity of these penetrating investigations were remarkable in that in the first half of the century the members of the committees and commissions which made them were not, as they would be today, drawn from or representative of the great bodies of the working classes. On the contrary, they were from the wealthy and ruling groups, for the composition of the House of Commons reflected the fact that even after the Reform Act of 1832 the number of voters was still but a tiny fraction of the adult population. The Northcote-Trevelyan proposals for the reform of the civil service by replacing recruitment by patronage with open competition, were approved by a cabinet all of whom, said Gladstone, who was a member of it, were more aristocratic than himself. No doubt they had their blind sides. For most of the century they assumed the existing class structure without much question; and there were fields in which their approach to problems and the conclusions they drew were influenced not only by the prevalent social philosophies, but class ideals and interests, as in the investigations into trade unions, game laws, etc. But the facts elicited in the examination of witnesses were not covered up or hidden — because apart from pressure by reforming groups, the constitutional procedure was that reports and evidence should be submitted and printed verbatim (see P. & G. Ford, *A Guide to Parliamentary Papers,* 3rd ed., IUP, 1972).

Further groups of papers are those which arose from the expansion of Britain overseas to control widely scattered colonial possessions and the development of areas of white settlement, Canada, Australia, and New Zealand. At the outset both kinds of territories were in some degree controlled from Whitehall. On the latter, beside formal committees of enquiry, there was a mass of despatches to and correspondence with colonial governors on the opening and sales of land for settlement, taxation, the administration of justice and the slow replacement of central control by primitive local representative bodies which eventually became the parliaments of self-governing dominions. In the case of the colonial possessions, after the Act abolishing slavery had been passed, the most striking feature was the immense body of papers which offer unique insight into the problem of enforcing this new political principle in widely scattered territories, differing in climate, crop conditions, land tenure, in the character and importance of slavery and in social structure. These are revealed in an immense volume of despatches, correspondence and instructions issued by the Colonial Office and the Foreign Office to colonial governors and their little Assemblies, which offered varying degrees of co-operation and resistance, and by the Admiralty in orders to commanders of naval vessels engaged all over the world in efforts to suppress the slave trade.

The great body of material for the nineteenth century occupies some 7,000 official folio volumes. At the outset the problem of making it available had to be met by the Printer to the House of Commons, Luke Hansard, who kept it in stock and numbered the House papers. He was frequently asked by M.P.s and others for sets of existing papers on particular questions then under discussion in the House or by the public. This led him to take two steps. He made special collections of papers arranged in subject order, and prepared a series of indexes to the papers, some in subject and some in alphabetical order. But the passage of a century has enlarged the number of papers to be handled and the scale of the problems; and at the same time we now have to meet the demand not only of the politician concerned with the problems of his time, but those of professional historians and researchers ranging over the whole century.

To deal with the papers on Home Affairs the Fords' *Select List of British Parliamentary Papers 1833-99* includes 4,000 policy papers arranged in subject order, so that researchers can follow the development lines of policy easily through any collection of papers. But complete collections are few and far between and even ample ones not common. The Irish University Press Parliamentary Papers series supplies this deficiency first by reprinting all the major policy papers, conveniently brought together in subject sets, e.g. 32 volumes on Agriculture, 44 volumes on Industrial Relations, 15 volumes on Children's Employment, 55 volumes on Education, and so on. Secondly, it has retained what was the great virtue of the original enquiries by reprinting with the reports all the volumes of evidence. Thirdly, in those fields where despatches, correspondence and instructions are vital as in the case of the papers on slavery, Canada, Australia, New Zealand, as far as possible all the papers on these matters found in the British Parliamentary series have been reprinted, e.g. 95 volumes on Slavery, 36 on Canada, 34 on Australia.

The series includes the most commonly used official general alphabetical indexes from which researchers can trace papers referred to in the footnotes of scholarly works and in the references in parliamentary reports themselves. In addition to the official indexes, a special index[1] to the 1,000 volumes has been prepared which will also provide cross references, so that the official indexes can be used either with the official sessional sets or with the IUP reprints.

1 *Checklist of British Parliamentary Papers in the Irish University Press 1000-Volume Series 1801-1899* (Shannon: 1972).

POPULATION

The Census, Great Britain and Ireland,
1801-1891

D. V. Glass

Contents

POPULATION

Preface

The account, which follows, of the nineteenth-century Censuses of Great Britain and Ireland is intended solely as a brief and general introduction. It is not a substitute for the much more detailed study by L. M. Feery, *Census Reports of Great Britain 1801-1931* — a study indispensable for anyone who wishes to use the censuses — and in the main deals with rather different aspects from those with which Feery's study is rightly concerned. Further, because the Irish University Press reprints do not include the first four censuses of Great Britain, other than in so far as their results are summarized in the *Comparative Account* of 1831, rather more space is given to those earlier censuses than might be justified by their importance as contributions to population statistics. For the rest, in using any given census, it is essential to look at the schedules applied and the procedures followed in collecting the basic statistics. And when the original returns or the enumerators' transcripts are available, they may be of additional help in showing how the instructions were actually carried out.

I am indebted to Dr. R. E. Jones, who helped to collect the material on which this account is based and who compiled the lists of Census Acts and of the published Census reports given in the Appendix. I am also grateful to Dr. W. S. Pickering for a number of references to modern studies of the 1851 religious census.

D. V. Glass

Commentary

The Census, Great Britain and Ireland, 1801-91

The 1801 Census: Background

The 1801 Census, the first of the periodic, official enumerations of the population of Great Britain, was undertaken at the end of extensive discussions which had begun in the middle of the eighteenth century. It was by no means the first attempt to collect population statistics in Britain. Local enumerations had had a long history, one such enumeration − of Ealing (London) − having been undertaken in 1599,[1] and there was a marked spread of local counts during the second half of the eighteenth century, to a considerable extent in response to the debate on whether the population had declined since the Glorious Revolution of 1688. In addition, various attempts had been made to estimate the total population. One of the better known − and possibly the most realistic − was Alexander Webster's estimate of the population of Scotland in 1755.[2] The estimates for England and Wales used a variety of techniques, but were in the main either based upon tax statistics or upon a combination of such statistics with local counts and local data on baptisms and burials. There was even an official enumeration − in some areas, more than one − in connection with the 1694 Act tax on marriages, births and burials, though whether there was in fact a full national coverage is not known. Only fragments of that enumeration survive, the largest collection of data being for eighty parishes of the City of London; and it was by using similar fragments, together with the statistics of the Hearth Tax, that Gregory King arrived at his famous estimate of the population of England and Wales in 1696.[3]

The pioneer days of political arithmetic − the period covering the writings of John Graunt, Sir William Petty and Gregory King, from the 1660s to the end of the seventeenth century − saw no official efforts to

1 K. J. Allison, *An Elizabethan 'Census' of Ealing* (Ealing Local History Society, 1962).

2 First fully published in J. G. Kyd, ed., *Scottish Population Statistics including Webster's Analysis of Population 1755* (Edinburgh, 1952). See also A. J. Youngson, 'Alexander Webster and his account of the number of people in Scotland in the year 1755', *Population Studies*, November 1961.

3 The data yielded by the 1694 Act are discussed in my introduction to W. Kellaway, ed., *London Inhabitants within the Walls 1695* (London, 1966). References to other publications assessing Gregory King's demographic work will be found in that introduction. King's writings are still largely unpublished.

establish regular censuses though it is possible that the 1694 Act had statistical as well as fiscal aims. But the population question was 'in the air', so to speak — on the Continent as well as in Britain — and with it a growing recognition that not only was there a lack of reliable population statistics but that the vital statistics supplied by the parochial registration system were seriously defective. That system, introduced in 1538 by an injunction of Thomas Cromwell, was supposed to cover the members of the Anglican community, though attempts were made to extend registration to the whole population during the Commonwealth and again under the 1694 Act. Large numbers of Dissenters were not covered by the parochial system, and Dissent grew during the eighteenth century. In addition, the system was seriously defective even in respect of the population it was supposed to cover. Many children were only 'half-baptised' — their baptisms took place in their homes and were not followed by public baptisms and a recording in the parish register. Children who died before baptism were often excluded from both the records of baptisms and of burials. And the clergy and their lay assistants were not infrequently both lax and dilatory in recording the events which came within their area of responsibility and of which they were presumably aware. There were many contemporary complaints of the deficiencies of the ecclesiastical registration system in respect of supplying vital statistics and records for inheritance purposes, and similar complaints of the omissions and errors in the Bills of Mortality for London, published by the Company of Parish Clerks. Precisely how defective the system was we do not know, but modern estimates suggest that by the 1820s — by which period there had been further deterioration associated both with urban expansion and with the growth of Dissent — the under-reporting of births and deaths amounted to 20 per cent or more.[4]

During the eighteenth century there were at least three attempts to improve vital registration, the best known aiming at a comprehensive system of demographic statistics, including censuses. This was the attempt embodied in the 1753 Bill, introduced by Thomas Potter, M.P. for St. Germans, Cornwall; a Bill for 'taking and registering an annual account of

4   An interesting evaluation of the under-registration of births in England and Wales in the late eighteenth and early nineteenth century is given in P. E. Razzell, 'Evaluation of baptism as a form of birth registration', *Population Studies*, 26, 1, 1972. R. E. Jones has provided a very detailed and imaginative assessment of the under-registration of births and deaths in one area in his Ph.D. thesis — *Parish Registers and Population History: North Shropshire, 1538-1837*, University of London, 1973. He estimates that in the late eighteenth and early nineteenth century, some 32 per cent of births and 25 per cent of deaths were omitted from the parish registers. My own work on the data for the City of London suggested that in 1696 some 25 per cent of births and 21 per cent of deaths were omitted from the London registers.

the total number of people, and of the total number of marriages, births and deaths, and also of the total number of the poor receiving alms from every Parish and Extra-parochial Place in Great Britain'. Had this Bill become law, we should have had a system of demographic statistics comparable to that established in Sweden in 1749 and still basically in force in that country today — though whether the law would have been effective here, given the quality of local administration, is doubtful. But the Bill did not become law: indeed it is remembered today less for the arguments in its favour than for the attacks on it, and especially the attack by William Thornton, M.P. for the City of York, who held that it would be 'totally subversive of the last remains of English liberty'. In spite of these attacks the Bill was passed in the House of Commons. But it was allowed to lapse in the House of Lords and no attempt was made to reintroduce it.[5]

But after the 1750s circumstances changed. The population controversy — and especially the debate in the 1780s between the Reverend Richard Price, who believed that there had been a fall in numbers, and William Wales and the Reverend John Howlett, who believed that numbers had increased — made a wider public aware of the deficiencies of existing statistics. There were many local enumerations, showing that censuses could be taken, while other countries took national censuses — Austria and Hungary, for example, Sweden, Holland and Spain and, in 1790, the U.S.A. Partly because of the increasing burden of poor relief, the earlier mercantilist view of the advantages of a growing population gradually gave way to fears of excessive growth, these fears being crystallized in Malthus's *Essay,* the first edition of which appeared in 1798. In addition, it had become necessary to import food, the result, many believed, of population increase. The food situation was especially difficult at the end of the century, with the disastrous summer and the very poor harvest of 1800, when wheat prices rose to 120/- per quarter and potatoes, potato flour and rice had to be used as substitutes for bread. A memorandum on 'the utility and facility of a general enumeration of the people of the British Empire', had been written by John Rickman, a friend of Charles Lamb, in 1796 and had been forwarded, through George Rose, M.P., to Charles Abbot, M.P. for Helston (Cornwall). Abbot must have been favourably impressed by the memorandum, for when he became Chief Secretary and Privy Seal in Ireland, he appointed Rickman to be his personal secretary. It was Abbot who introduced the Population Bill in the House of Commons in 1800,

---

5 The eighteenth century debate on population and on census and vital statistics is discussed in D. V. Glass, *Numbering the People* (Farnborough, 1973). I have drawn generally on that book in dealing with the early history of the British censuses and shall not refer to specific pages.

some of the provisions in the Bill reflecting Rickman's proposals, and the Bill was passed on 31 December 1800 – an 'Act for taking an Account of the Population of Great Britain, and of the Increase or Diminution thereof'. The actual enumeration took place on 10 March 1801, the first of the official, periodic censuses of Great Britain, the population being required by law to furnish the information requested in the schedules.

Ireland

The Census Act of 1800 provided for enumerations in England and Wales and Scotland. Ireland was not included in the prescribed coverage, perhaps because it was believed that census taking would be more difficult in that country. It was certainly not due to lack of interest in the growth of the population of Ireland, a subject on which there had been considerable speculation, and in respect of which various estimates had been put forward and some valuable local enumerations carried out.[6] But the success of the 1801 Census of Britain may have inspired the Bill for taking a census of Ireland, introduced in the House of Commons in 1806, but defeated at the first reading. The exclusion of Ireland from the general enumeration was again discussed in the House of Commons during the debate, in January 1812, on the 1811 Census of Great Britain and another Bill introduced, becoming law on 18 July 1812 and providing for an enumeration to be begun on 1 May 1813. In fact, however, the 1812 'Act for taking an Account of the Population of Ireland, and of the Increase or Diminution thereof', did not result in the first effective census of Ireland. The administrative structure was inappropriate and unsatisfactory. The supervision of the work was entrusted to the grand juries and the enumeration was carried out by the constables in the counties and by various parish officers in the main cities and towns. The constables were disliked and distrusted. Religious affiliation – that is, Protestant – being often their only ground for appointment, they were poor enumerators. And in any case there was unrest in Ireland and considerable antagonism to the census, and not only from Roman Catholics. When in March 1815 the enumeration was declared to be ended, it was in fact incomplete, while many of the returns which had been submitted were unsatisfactory. In anticipation of the 1821 Census therefore, new administrative arrangements were prescribed by an Act of 1815, under which the Magistrates at the Quarter Sessions and the Assistant Barristers were charged with

6   One of the most interesting local enumerations in Ireland was that of Dublin in 1798. See Rev. James Whitelaw, *An Essay on the Population of Dublin* (Dublin, 1805). For a general discussion of estimates of the population of Ireland, see K. H. Connell, *The Population of Ireland* (Oxford, 1950), Chapter 1.

superintending the next Census. There were still problems in 1821. Nevertheless the 1821 Census returns were far more satisfactory than those of 1813, and the full census results were published in 1823.[7] The 1821 Census was thus in reality the first of the periodic censuses of Ireland.

Responsibility; Enumeration Techniques and Analysis

Initially, the censuses in Great Britain and Ireland were undertaken on an *ad hoc* basis. There was no permanent census organization and each census was preceded by a specific and separate Act of Parliament; the latter circumstance continued to apply in Britain until the 1920 Census Act, which provided for regular decennial censuses and which also allowed for the possibility of a quinquennial census, a possibility not translated into action until 1966. It was perhaps not surprising that the task of organizing the 1801 Census of Great Britain was entrusted to John Rickman – he certainly considered himself to be the instigator of that census. 'At my suggestion they have passed an Act of Parliament for ascertaining the population of Great Britain', he wrote to Southey in 1800, 'and as a compliment (of course) have proposed me to superintend the execution of it'.[8] He was effective in the sense that the census was completed and the results digested and published speedily – two volumes were ordered to be printed in 1801 and the third in 1802 – and he continued to take responsibility for the next three censuses, namely those of 1811, 1821 and 1831. The enumerators were overseers of the poor in England and Wales, with assistance from various church officials and, if need be, from the 'constables, tithingmen, headboroughs or other peace officers'. In Scotland the work was done by schoolmasters or 'other fit persons'. But a permanent body was created under the 1836 Act, which introduced civil vital registration. Various committees dealing with Friendly Societies had made it clear that the data used for calculating mortality rates and for constructing life tables were generally inadequate and parliament was made aware of the fact that the Dissenters were to a considerable extent

7   P. Froggatt, 'The census in Ireland of 1813-15', *Irish Historical Studies*, Vol. XIV, No. 55, March 1965; M. Greenwood and P. Granville Edge, *Official Vital Statistics of Ireland* (League of Nations Health Organisation, Geneva, 1929); Census of Ireland, *1901: General Report*, pp. 1-3. See also H. Wood, 'Methods of registering and estimating the population of Ireland before 1864,' *Journal of the Statistical and Social Inquiry Society of Ireland*, Vol. 12, Part 89, December 1909. An account of the 1813 Census, with a summary of the main results, is given in W. S. Mason, *A Statistical Account or Parochial Survey of Ireland*, Vol. 3 (Dublin, 1819), pp. xxii-xlv. At the 1821 census the enumerators were generally local tax collectors whose qualifications were examined by the magistrates. The data were tabulated centrally and not locally, as had been done in 1813.

8   Orlo Williams, *Life and Letters of John Rickman* (London, 1911), p. 38.

excluded from the parish registers and that for Anglicans, too, the coverage was far from complete. The deficiencies of the existing ecclesiastical system were fully displayed in 1833 in the Report of the Select Committee on Parochial Registration. It was to remedy these defects that the 1836 Act was passed, and the new civil system was put under the administration of a General Register Officer, with a Registrar General at its head. It was natural that the Registrar General should take a major share of the responsibility for the Census. He was one of three commissioners appointed to take the 1841 Census and from 1851 onwards he took charge of the census, with the registrars of marriages, births and deaths as his agents directing the enumeration in their districts. When, under the 1854 Act, civil vital registration was introduced into Scotland the responsibility for the subsequent Scottish censuses passed to the Registrar General of Scotland and the censuses from 1861 to 1891 inclusive were covered by separate Acts for Scotland. It was not until 1901 that a single Act, covering Great Britain, again became the rule. In Ireland, *ad hoc* arrangements were made in 1831 and 1841, with three Commissioners responsible for the latter census. But from 1851 onwards the censuses became the responsibility of a Census Commission, with the Registrar General, appointed under the 1844 Act for the registration of marriages in Ireland, as the Chief Commissioner.[9]

Although the reports of the early censuses do not display in detail the way in which the enumeration was conducted in each locality, it is clear that a heavy burden fell upon the enumerators and other local personnel. The census returns had to be made in a 'prescribed form', to be sent via the Clerks to the Peace or the Town Clerks to the Home Secretary. That prescribed form was in effect a digest for the area, based upon the information collected personally by the enumerators from each household. The enumerator was thus in effect largely an interviewer, but exactly how he had to record the information is not specified and there may well have been considerable variation.[10] The returns sent to the Home Office by

9   The 1844 Act dealt only with marriages and for non-Catholics. Civil vital registration as such was introduced under the 1863 Act, subsequently modified by the Births and Deaths Act of 1880.

10   Although the 1801 census placed the responsibility for collecting the prescribed information on the overseers of the poor and other specified persons, there was evidently some variation in practice. Thus the surviving local schedules for Hampstead − they are printed forms, issued over the name of the Vestry Clerk − suggest that they were distributed in advance to the householders who were expected to complete them, one form for each household. The instruction at the bottom of the printed forms reads: 'The Overseers particularly request that the respective Inhabitants of this Parish will correctly fill up the above Columns, and preserve this Notice until called for, which will be on the 10th Day of March, 1801.' (The schedules for Hampstead for 1801 and 1811 are in the possession of the Borough of Camden − at the Central Library, Swiss Cottage).

each locality no longer exist – they were destroyed in 1931 – so that it is not possible to tell how much additional digesting, except in the form of summaries for hundreds, counties and the country as a whole, was done centrally. And there was no provision for keeping the local returns in the localities of origin, so that it is a matter of chance that returns for a few areas have survived. What seems evident is that, for the most part, the local returns could scarcely have been checked for reliability, in spite of the fact that those returns had to be sworn to before the Justices of the Peace, for there was apparently no listing of individuals by name. Households were listed, and the membership of each household summarized – for example, in 1801 by sex and by broad occupational category, namely, in agriculture; in trade, manufacture, or handicraft; and in all other categories. Judging from the returns for Croydon, the 1811 census returns were recorded in the same way. On each line of the list there is a summary for a particular house, e.g. John Tubbs, bricklayer, three males, two females, total five, and there is no evidence to suggest that the summary was based on a prior listing of every individual. At the 1821 Census the process appears to have been somewhat different, at least to judge from the returns available for Braintree (Essex). A question on age, to be answered on a voluntary basis, was included in the 1821 schedule, and the Braintree returns suggest that the preparation of the digest sent to London was carried out in two stages. There was first a listing of every individual in each house, the 'exact' age of each individual being given, but the names of only the householders (and sometimes of a lodger). The age data were then summarized (separately for males and females) on another set of sheets, one line being allocated to each house. All this was done on ordinary paper, not on printed forms. It seems to have been left to the local area to decide whether or not to print forms – Croydon, for example, did provide sheets with printed headings for the 1811 Census. For the 1831 Census, however, there was a centrally printed form entitled 'Formula for taking and preparing the account of the resident population', again with each line summarizing the data for a house. In addition, the enumerators were supplied with special 'tally sheets' to help them to make more reliable counts and summaries.

A radical change in census arrangements took place with the establishment of the General Register Office. Initially, Rickman drew up plans for the 1841 Census, on lines similar to those of the earlier censuses, and these plans were reflected in the first Census Bill of 1840. But the London (afterwards Royal) Statistical Society had appointed a Committee to put forward proposals for the 1841 census, and that committee, whose report was published in April 1840, recommended a fundamental change in census procedure – the adoption of a household schedule listing the names and characteristics of each individual enumerated – and a much wider range of questions. The committee's report was sent to the Home Secretary and there must have been a good deal of lobbying, for the original Bill was withdrawn and an amended Bill, embodying many of the committee's recommendations, was introduced and passed in August 1840. An amending Act of April 1841 took the change still further by providing that, in addition to the new schedules for the enumerators, an additional householder's schedule should be distributed to every householder a few days before the census date. The 1841 Census thus represented the first use in Britain of a self-administered household schedule, listing by name and characteristics every individual in the household. The enumerators ceased to be interviewers, though they no doubt had to give considerable help to householders, many of whom would have been illiterate, in completing their schedules. In addition, the area basis of the enumeration was shifted from the parishes and townships of the earlier censuses to the registration districts of the new civil vital statistics system. Partly in order to ensure that the actual census count should be completed in one or two days, each registration district was divided into enumeration districts, designed to allow complete coverage by an enumerator in the specified time. And instead of local summaries of the census data being sent to London for further digesting and publication, the whole analysis of the basic data — that is, of the data relating the members of every household and institution — was centralized in the General Register Office.

Exactly who at the newly established General Register Office was responsible for all these changes is not known. The first Registrar General, T. H. Lister, was not an administrator: the brother-in-law of Lord John Russell, he was a novelist. But in 1839 he had appointed William Farr as Compiler of Abstracts. Farr, one of the most distinguished demographers of the nineteenth century, was initially concerned primarily with vital statistics as such, though he was also Assistant Commissioner at the censuses of 1851, 1861 and 1871. But he may well have been consulted on the preparations for the census. A manuscript memorandum in the library of the General Register Office gives an account of those preparations, which included a pilot survey to assess the number of households an enumerator would be able to cover, as well as an unsuccessful attempt to ascertain the local costs of the 1831 Census.[11] For anyone interested in the detailed planning of a census, the memorandum is a most interesting

11   The memorandum of 142 pages is entitled *History of the Census of 1841*. No author's name is given, and no date of completion, though the memorandum was evidently written after the death of T. H. Lister (in 1842). It was apparently not secrecy or corruption which defeated the attempt to discover the costs of the 1831 enumeration. With the change in local administration brought in with the 1834 Poor Law, many of the old records were destroyed. In addition, some of the enumerators worked voluntarily or were paid in kind — e.g. by being given a dinner.

document, and one that has a wider relevance than the title would suggest, for in respect of essential techniques the 1841 Census acted as the model for all subsequent nineteenth-century British censuses and for the censuses of Ireland, too.[12]

One aspect of census taking remained basically unchanged, namely the manual tabulation of the data. The transfer of the analysis from the local district to the centre no doubt reduced the frequency of errors, especially as from 1841 onwards the tabulation was based upon the detailed information for each individual and not, as in earlier censuses, upon local summaries which could not be checked. But manual tabulation imposed constraints upon the use of the data. Even with modern computer analysis of tapes, census data are never fully utilized; hence the increasing practice of supplying duplicate tapes − provided that individuals cannot be identified − for use by local authorities and research workers or of making special arrangements for the purchase of additional tabulations. The cross-tabulations published in the reports of the nineteenth century censuses were far more limited in scope, and some of the important topics of the day were discussed without the assistance which might have been provided by a fuller analysis of the census returns. The employment of married women is one such topic, and it was often discussed, not only as part of the continuing debate on opportunities for women and on 'the subjection of women', but also in connection with infant mortality. The cotton famine during the American Civil War was widely regarded as contributing to the fall in infant mortality in Lancashire. Married women who were thrown out of employment were able to devote more attention to their children and to dispense with the services of 'baby minders'. From 1851 onwards the British Censuses collected information on employment by age, sex and marital condition, but the relevant cross-tabulations were first supplied at the 1901 Census.[13] And this lack of cross-tabulations

12   Like the British census, the 1841 Census of Ireland, which was also the subject of an amending Act, used a household schedule.

13   The question of the consequences of the employment of married women was examined by Dr. M. Hewitt in her Ph.D. thesis (University of London 1953) on *The Effect of Married Women's Employment in the Cotton Textile Districts on the Home in Lancashire, 1840-1880,* a revised version of which was published under the title of *Wives and Mothers in Victorian Industry* (London, 1958). The thesis was based in part upon the analysis of the data in the enumerators' transcript books for samples of households in several areas at several points of time and represented one of the first studies to use such data. For a good example of Victorian writing on employment opportunities for women, see J. D. Milne, *Industrial Employment of Women in the Middle and Lower Ranks.* (Revised edn. London, 1870. The first edition was published anonymously in 1857.) There was also considerable discussion of employment opportunities for middle-class spinsters − the 'surplus women' of Victorian Britain. For a survey of some aspects of that discussion see A. Deacon and M. Hill, 'The problem of "Surplus Women" in the nineteenth century: secular and religious alternatives', *A Sociological Yearbook of Religion in Britain,* 5 (London, 1972).

applied to a wide range of topics, so that the enumerators' transcript books — those for the 1841, 1851 and 1861 censuses are now accessible at the Public Record Office, and the 1871 Census returns should also soon be available — are a mine of information on the demographic and social conditions of mid-nineteenth-century Britain.[14] The limitations of existing tabulations were known to contemporaries and they were discussed in the 1890 report of the Treasury Committee on the Census.[15] But mechanical processing of the data by punched cards was not used until the 1911 Census, which was thereby able to provide for more detailed analyses. The shift to mechanized data processing also involved a further change in the procedure for analysing census data. Before 1911, it was not the original schedules which were analysed, but the copies of them in the enumerators' transcript books. Henceforth the data were coded directly from the schedules, and this may have resulted in some further gain in accuracy by eliminating one more intermediate stage.

The Scope of the Census

The questions covered by a census almost always represent a compromise between conflicting demands. Various groups (both official and private) are anxious to obtain information bearing upon their fields of interest, and the longer the experience of censuses, the more the demands for information appear to grow. Some groups, on the other hand, press for the exclusion of certain types of question. In the U.S.A., for example, Congress, no doubt influenced by the views of some of the more articulate voters, has refused to allow questions on religious affiliation to be included. In Britain, at the time of the 1971 Census, there was concern about a proposed question on income and the question was removed and transferred to the post-enumeration survey, the response to which would

14 During the past few years there has been a very considerable expansion in the use of these basic census data. An interesting recent example is M. Anderson, *Family Structure in Nineteenth Century Lancashire* (Cambridge, 1971). See also W. A. Armstrong, 'A note on the household structure of mid-nineteenth century York in comparative perspective', in P. Laslett, ed., *Household and Family in Past Time* (Cambridge, 1972). (In the U.S.A., too, there has also been a marked increase in the use of the basic data of the nineteenth-century American censuses).

15 *Report of the Committee appointed by the Treasury to inquire into Certain Questions connected with the Taking of the Census,* London 1890, BPP, 1890, Vol. LVIII. The committee, of which Charles Booth was a member, was appointed as a result of a delegation to the Board of Trade in 1888. Quinquennial censuses were recommended, the mid-decennial census to ascertain age and sex (there had been considerable complaint about the unreliability of intercensal estimates of local populations). The Treasury was also urged to give further consideration to the use of mechanical tabulation (the committee had been sent documents by Herman Hollerith, whose electro-mechanical system had been adopted for processing the 1890 Census data in the U.S.A.).

be on a voluntary basis. The type of question objected to differs between countries. Many countries, for example, have consistently included questions on religion in their censuses, while others have frequently included questions on income. On these areas of inquiry demographers and statisticians rarely have the last word, for the interests of particular pressure groups are too closely involved. Where the technical advisers have more influence is in respect of feasibility. Some subjects, for example, can only be dealt with by the inclusion of a series of questions, and that may be ruled out, given the total number of questions considered to be practicable in a full enumeration. (In modern censuses such subjects may be dealt with in a supplementary schedule distributed to only a sample of the population). There is also the question of the literacy of the population being enumerated and the related question of the quality of the enumerators. John Rickman did not have a high opinion of the overseers of the poor as enumerators and was insistent that they should not have to deal with an elaborate schedule. In the mid-nineteenth century, on the other hand, the enumerators tended to be praised. The General Report on the 1861 Census of England and Wales listed the qualities to be looked for in the enumerators: they 'were required to be intelligent and active, able to read and write well, not younger than 18 years of age or older than 60; they were to be respectable persons likely to conduct themselves with strict propriety and courtesy in the discharge of their duties, and well acquainted with the district in which they were to act.' And the Report added: 'No difficulty was experienced in procuring the services of a highly respectable body of enumerators, including clergymen and many other professional men who undertook the work from public motives.' But in giving evidence to the subsequent Treasury Committee on the Census, Dr. William Ogle, of the General Register Office, expressed a much less favourable view — 'Well, they are on the whole a rather poor lot,' he said. Of course, the pay was very low — an average of £1.14.3$\frac{1}{2}$ per enumerator for a week's work at the previous census. Nevertheless, he doubted whether it would be possible to 'collect an army of 35,000, or perhaps in 1891 of 40,000, really good men for a temporary purpose.'[16] The question of cost, referred to in the discussion of Dr. Ogle's evidence, is clearly also an important factor in limiting the scope of a census, and often much more so in the case of regular statistical inquiries like the periodic enumerations than for *ad hoc* investigations

16   Dr. Ogle appears to have been pessimistic about other branches of demographic statistics. When he gave evidence to the Select Committee on Death Certification of 1893-94 he argued that the registration of stillbirths, for which many groups and experts had pressed, would be impracticable. Stillbirth registration did not take place until 1927 in England and Wales and 1939 in Scotland (the 1874 Act provided for notification of stillbirths but not their registration).

sponsored by Royal Commissions. Naturally cost has to be taken into account and that is one of the considerations involved when deciding whether to conduct inquiries by sampling instead of on a 100 per cent basis.[17] But if cost becomes a fetish, the quality of the enumeration may be so poor that the results are of little value, so that the apparently low cost turns out to be very expensive. In fact that did not happen in Britain, even though the costs of the actual enumeration amounted to only £5. 3. 11 per 1,000 of the population in 1851 and to only £4. 3. 2 per 1,000 persons in 1891.[18] But the apparently still lower cost in Ireland — with the police being used as enumerators — was one of the factors cited in explanation of the inclusion of religion in the schedule and may help to explain the generally far wider range of subjects covered by the Irish censuses, though it was no doubt not the sole reason.

At the 1801 Census, with no experience upon which to draw and no evidence to suggest that the practice of other countries with such experience was considered, the schedule was very brief. The enumerators collected information on the numbers of males and females, of families, of inhabited and vacant houses, and of persons engaged in two broad categories of employment. In addition, there were questions to be answered by the clergy, who had to supply from the parish registers statistics of marriages, baptisms and burials for specified periods — marriages for each year from 1754 to 1800, and baptisms and burials for each year from 1780 to 1800 and for every tenth year from 1700 to 1780. The information collected by the enumerators provided a very elementary outline picture of the population. The parish register statistics were designed to be used — and were so used by Rickman — in estimating the population of England and Wales during the eighteenth century. William Morgan, actuary to the Equitable Life Assurance Society, criticized the 1801 Census for its limitations. He said that: 'It appears to have been instituted for the mere purpose of determining a controversy; and even in this it has totally failed of its object'. His comments were influenced by his desire to defend the memory of his uncle, the Reverend Richard Price. The historical statistics of marriages, baptisms and burials were collected in an

---

17   But naturally only *one* of the factors. There is also the question of the practical (as distinct from the theoretical) difficulties involved in taking an appropriate sample, as well as possible objections by the public to being 'selected' for questioning. Problems of this kind sometimes arise when a 100 per cent enumeration is supplemented by a more detailed schedule addressed to a sample of the population.

18   1921 Census of England and Wales, *General Report*, London 1927. The amounts represented expenditure under the census vote, excluding the cost of printing, stationery, maps, cards and the hire of machines. At the 1921 Census the cost was £9. 5. 6. per 1,000 population, the increase stated to be due entirely to the higher cost of living.

attempt to estimate population growth during the eighteenth century, a matter not merely of academic interest but also of practical concern in assessing the causes of the apparent inadequacy of home food production. Nevertheless Morgan was justified in claiming that the 1801 Census should — and probably could — have asked for more information, and in particular on the ages of the people. The returns on ages would undoubtedly have contained numerous errors, but this applied almost as much when age came to be included as a regular question in the censuses from 1841 onwards. And even flawed age statistics would have given additional help in studying the trend of fertility in Britain during the first half of the nineteenth century.

Rickman was in charge of the censuses from 1801 to 1831 inclusive. He had a relatively low opinion of overseers of the poor as agents of the enumeration. Initially, too, he had little appreciation of the importance of various kinds of demographic data, though he tried to study some of the technical literature and, according to his son, translated Deparcieux's work on mortality. It was perhaps as a result of such study that he gave up the erroneous approach to life table construction which had formed the basis of some of his early articles on the population of Britain. At any rate, his view of the needs and practical possibilities of census taking was rather conservative. He undertook pilot surveys to examine alternative questions on occupation, and he included a question on age in the schedule of the 1821 Census, the question to be asked on a voluntary basis. Enumerators were asked to ascertain ages if they could be obtained 'in a manner satisfactory to yourself, and not inconvenient to the Parties. . . .' But there was little other improvement in the census schedules and some deterioration in 1811 when the question on personal occupation was replaced by one on family occupation. And although age was included in 1821, Rickman was strongly opposed to its repetition in 1831. The Committee on the 1830 Population Bill had received evidence from Joshua Milne, the most distinguished actuary of his day and the author of the Carlisle Life Table, the first realistic English life table. Milne had explained that the correct construction of life tables required statistics of the population by age as well as deaths by age. Rickman, who clearly misunderstood Milne's evidence, rejected it. The 1831 Census did not go beyond asking for the numbers of males over twenty years of age, and the enumerators were told that if this was substantially different from one half of the total number of males, or in other ways as compared with the 1821 returns, '. . . some Error has probably been committed, and the Answer to this Question should be examined, and corrected if necessary.' The rhythm of a decennial census was accepted by Rickman; he did not believe that shorter intervals between censuses were either necessary or justifiable.

The collection of parish register data on marriages, baptisms and burials for England and Wales was continued by Rickman in connection with each census, and he attempted to include data for Dissenters. For the period prior to the implementation of the 1836 Act on civil vital registration, these are the only available vital statistics to cover the whole of England and Wales, though they are undoubtedly defective. Under the Rose Act of 1812, ages at death were reported in the parish registration system and Rickman had those data collected for the period 1813-30 and published as part of the 1831 Census returns. In addition, the returns include a table of illegitimate births in 1830, also based upon statistics supplied by the clergy. Finally, in an effort to provide population estimates going back to the sixteenth century, in 1836 Rickman circularized the clergy of those parishes which possessed old registers and asked for the numbers of marriages, baptisms and burials for three-year periods centred on six points of time – namely 1570, 1600, 1630, 1670, 1700 and 1750. The estimates of population based upon those statistics – the estimates assume the constancy of the ratios of marriages, baptisms and burials to the total population at the levels computed for 1801 – were printed posthumously in the 1841 Census publications.[19]

With the establishment of the General Register Office and the appointment of registrars and superintendent registrars to operate the system of civil vital registration, it also became possible to use the new organization to take charge of the censuses. The General Register Office, under lay Registrars General, had some technically qualified staff, beginning with William Farr, and its non-technical staff gradually gained relevant knowledge through practical experience. Further, the registrars were certainly much better able than the overseers of the poor to supervise the enumeration in their districts: in the early days of civil registration, over 500 of the registrars were medically qualified. The population in general became more accustomed to censuses – at no time was there widespread antagonism in Britain – and various expert groups pressed for additional questions to be included in the schedules. The London (afterwards Royal) Statistical Society was one such group, and before each census it appointed a committee to make recommendations for the next

19 On Rickman's estimates and other population estimates based upon the parish register statistics, see my paper on 'Population and population movements in England and Wales, 1700 to 1850', in D. V. Glass and D. E. C. Eversley, *Population History* (London, 1965). Scotland was excluded from the collection of parish register data on the grounds that the registers for that part of the Kingdom were few and poor. They were, though perhaps not quite so few or poor as was believed at the time. (Professor Michael Flinn and his colleagues at Edinburgh University have recently been analysing the data in the available registers.) After 1841, with civil vital statistics available and analysed in substantial annual reports, the collection of parish register statistics was given up.

census.[20] It was the first of those committees which in 1840 pressed for a radical change in the 1841 Census, and several of its recommendations were accepted, notably the listing by name of every individual in a house, with sex, age, occupation and birthplace, though others were not, including relationship to the head of the household, marital condition and religious persuasion.[21] The 1850 committee proposed that schools should be covered by the census, that the average weekly attendance during a period prior to the enumeration should be reported and that there should be a statement of the numbers of pupils, by age and sex, on the books on census day.[22] The recommendations of the 1860 committee included – in addition to education and religion, covered to some extent in 1851 – greater age detail for children under five, a range of agricultural statistics, and as far as possible, common schedules and published analyses for the censuses of Great Britain and Ireland.[23] Religion and education were again proposed in the 1870 and 1880 recommendations, and questions on housing were put forward. In addition, the 1870 committee urged that there should be information on the ability to read or write (for individuals above the age of seven). The 1880 committee proposed, too, that there should be quinquennial censuses, the census for the mid-point of the decade to collect at least information on the number of houses and the number and ages of the population; and that there should be overall census reports for the United Kingdom, to include not only census analyses but also special reports by appropriate government departments on such topics as education, pauperism and crime.[24] The quinquennial census proposal was endorsed by the Treasury Committee and again put forward by the 1890 Committee of the Royal Statistical Society, though, as mentioned earlier, it was not until 1966 that the first quinquennial census was taken.[25]

20   In putting forward proposals the committees took into account the census practices of other countries. The report of the 1840 committee contains much information on these practices.

21   *Journal of the Statistical Society of London (J.R.S.S.)*, Vol. 3, 1840, pp. 72-102.

22   *J.R.S.S.*, Vol. 13, 1850, pp. 267-269.

23   *J.R.S.S.*, Vol. 23, 1860, pp. 222-223.

24   *J.R.S.S.*, Vol. 33, 1870, p. 113 and Vol. 43, 1880, pp. 134-139. The 1880 proposals were generally in agreement with those put forward by the National Association for the Promotion of Social Science. In 1870 a committee of the British Association for the Advancement of Science had sent a memorandum to the Home Secretary, urging that there should be uniformity in conducting the census throughout the United Kingdom and also in the analysis and publication of the results (*J.R.S.S.*, Vol. 33, 1870, pp. 522-523).

25   *J.R.S.S.*, Vol. 51, 1888, pp. 816-818.

Some of the recommendations were accepted without serious difficulty and from 1851 onwards the census schedule regularly contained questions on sex, age, marital status, relationship to the head of the household, birthplace and nationality, personal occupation and infirmities. There were questions on unemployment in 1871 and 1881, and on the language spoken (Gaelic in Scotland from 1881, Welsh in Wales from 1891). Scotland, with the census carried out by her own Registrar General from 1861, included questions on windows in the houses enumerated and England and Wales collected information on the number of rooms per household from 1891. But some of the topics suggested aroused antagonism and this was especially so in respect of religion and, in a somewhat smaller degree, education. Indeed, much of the discussion in parliament, when proposals for the censuses from 1851 onwards came up for consideration, was concerned with questions on religion.[26] When the Registrar General included a question on attendance at Church, Chapel and other religious institutions in the 1851 schedule, there were various objections to the aim of making the question a compulsory one, with penalties for the clergy who failed to answer it; and those objections were supported by the government's legal advisers. In order to retain the question, the Registrar General agreed to allow the inquiry to be undertaken on a voluntary basis.[27] The results were criticized, especially as they showed a high attendance of non-conformists at their services.[28] But even stronger objections were raised when a question on religious persuasion was proposed for the 1861 Census, and especially objections from Dissenting groups, who obviously felt that they would make a poorer showing on religious persuasion than on religious attendance. The proposal

26   The main parliamentary discussions from 1841 to 1891 may be seen in the following issues of *Hansard* – the references are not necessarily exhaustive: *Hansard,* 3rd Series, 57(1841), Col. 397; 111(1850), Cols. 868-871; 114(1851), Cols. 1306-1310 and 1316-1317; 115(1851), Cols. 112-114 and 629-633; 158(1860), Cols. 91-93 and 1762-1766; 159(1860), Cols. 1695-1741; 160(1860), Cols. 78-82 and 82-83; 202(1870), Cols. 1356-1357 and 1711-1712; 203(1870), Cols. 806-818, 1002-1011, 1228-1230, 1399-1406, 1706 and 1730; 254(1880), Cols. 144-147, 465-467, 890-892, 1066-1069, 1196-1197, and 2072-2074; 255(1880), Cols. 747-756 and 861-867; 256(1880), Cols. 1063-1098; 343(1890), Cols. 1472-1475; 345(1890), Cols. 949-961; 347(1890), Cols. 399-429, 514-539, 910-911, 1524-1525, and 1722-1724; 348(1890), Cols. 20-46 and 920-922.

27   [L. M. Feery], *Census Reports of Great Britain 1801-1931,* Guides to Official Sources, No. 2 (London, 1951) p. 85.

28   Much of the criticism was replied to by Horace Mann, who was associated with the religious census. See H. Mann, 'On the statistical position of religious bodies in England and Wales', *J.R.S.S.,* Vol. 18, 1855, pp. 141-159. The 1851 religious census has continued, right up to the present, to serve as a basis of studies of the rôle of religion in nineteenth-century Britain and as a point of departure for the examination of more recent trends.

was withdrawn, though the government spokesman in the House of Commons explained that the question was included in the censuses of many countries. The 1871 Census did not include the question; it was not proposed by the government for the 1881 Census and a motion in the House of Commons was defeated; in 1890, the question was again rejected, this time by a large majority at the committee stage of the Census Bill.[29] In fact, at no census in Britain has the question been asked, though there have been many local and some national surveys of religious affiliation, attendance and belief, some of the surveys being extremely detailed in their enquiries into the significance of religion for the individuals interviewed.[30]

The comments on changes in the scope of the census have so far been confined to Britain. The Irish censuses need separate discussion, for the organization of these censuses was distinct and the scope often much wider.

After the abortive census of 1813-15, the 1821 and 1831 censuses were taken on lines similar to those in Britain and with a similar range of questions.[31] The organization was improved and there was less tension in the country between the governing and the governed. The censuses were thus more effective. The 1841 Census saw substantial changes. The recommendations of the Committee of the London Statistical Society and the amending of the initial Bill for the Census of Great Britain, had its repercussions on the plans for the Irish census. A three-man census commission was appointed and a household schedule prepared, going well beyond the British schedule in its scope. Questions were asked on sex, age (in great detail), relationship to the head of the household, marital status and date of marriage, occupation, ability to read or write, birthplace, education and school attendance and housing. In addition, as there were neither national parish register data (the bulk of the population would in any case have been excluded from such registers) nor civil vital statistics,

29 Michael Drake, basing his account on reports in *The Times,* has given an interesting survey of a wide range of proposals for and comments on the censuses. See M. Drake, 'The census, 1801-1891', in E. A. Wrigley, ed., *Nineteenth-century Society. Essays in the Use of Quantitative Methods for the Study of Social Data* (Cambridge, 1972). See also in the same volume, the chapter by B. I. Coleman, 'The incidence of education in mid-century'.

30 For example, I have been associated with two national sample surveys (of fertility and birth control practice) in which questions were asked about the religious affiliations of husbands and wives and also about the importance of religion to them.

31 But the 1821 Census reported the numbers attending school. In addition, although there was no household schedule, enumerators were required to write in their notebooks a detailed listing of the names, characteristics (but marital condition was not apparently generally required) and relationship to the head, of every individual in the household. Unfortunately, no copy of the 1831 schedule – or of the actual list of questions – has so far been found.

the census collected information on the marriages, births and deaths which had occurred during the previous ten years, showing them separately for each year.[32] (Deaths by cause were also collected from hospitals and other institutions and tabulated by sex and age). Whatever protests may have been made by the population of Ireland, parliament in London did not appear to raise objections to this very detailed enumeration.

At the 1851 Census the range of inquiry was still further extended. The household schedule had added to it questions on the use of the Irish language and on infirmities. And there were other schedules for collecting information on the number of persons who were ill on a specified day, on sickness among the inmates of various institutions and on the numbers of idiots and lunatics. On this occasion, the Chief Commissioner was the recently appointed Registrar General for Ireland, and an assistant commissioner had been added, to deal in particular with the vital statistics which were to be collected. The man appointed was William (later Sir William) Wilde, the father of Oscar Wilde, who achieved fame as an aural and an ophthalmic surgeon, earned distinction in several other fields, and notoriety in respect of his personal life. Wilde had been appointed at the 1841 Census to analyse the statistics of deaths during the previous ten years and his report had been well received. Working on a part-time basis and giving general assistance at the 1851 Census, he had special responsibility for data on mortality and morbidity and produced two major reports, *Status of Disease* and *Tables of Death*. It is remarkable that these reports in particular, and the census reports as a whole, were produced at a time when the Famine had only recently ended.[33] The subsequent censuses, from 1861 to 1891, saw little change Religious profession was added in 1861 and was retained thereafter, and the unemployed were enumerated in 1881 and 1891. But with the introduction of civil vital registration, the census ceased to collect information on births and deaths, and the date of marriage was also dropped after 1871. There was no major development until 1911 when, along with England and Wales and Scotland, the census of Ireland added questions on fertility — on the total number of children born alive to married women. The 1911 censuses are factually part of twentieth-century census history. But in

32   Death statistics were based on returns for each household, reporting 'members of the Family, Servants, or Visitors, who have *died while residing with this Family,* since the 6th June, 1831', together with cause of death. [1841 Census of Ireland, *Report of the Commissioners* (Dublin, 1843) p. xci.] The number of births were estimates constructed by combining the census data on children under ten with the reported deaths of children at the relevant ages during the proceeding ten years. On the probable errors in the estimates see G. S. L. Tucker, 'Irish Fertility Ratios before the Famine', *Economic History Review*, 2nd series, Vol. 33 No. 2, August 1970.

33   P. Froggatt, 'The demographic work of Sir William Wilde', *Ir. J. Med. Sc.*, May 1965. Wilde continued to act at the 1861 and 1871 censuses. He died in 1876.

many ways they may also be regarded as an extension of the nineteenth-century model. They are classic examples of their type and the type as such continued to be used until quite recently. But modern fertility censuses have departed considerably from that earlier pattern, as witness the 1971 censuses of Great Britain, with their different definition of the population to be enumerated,[34] their wide coverage of relevant variables to be cross-tabulated against fertility, and their much more detailed questions on fertility itself, involving the recording of the date of birth of each child born alive to a married woman.

The heads of inquiry mentioned in examining the changes in the census schedules during the nineteenth century do not exhaust the topics covered by the censuses. Students intending to use the censuses should consult Feery's study of British censuses,[35] which gives much more detail, including an analysis of the areas for which tabulations were provided. In addition, when it became customary to publish general reports on the censuses — from 1861 onwards — these reports often contained material not found in other volumes. And those other volumes also not infrequently presented material outside the main categories of analysis, such as the various estimates by Rickman, Finlaison and Farr of the course of population during the eighteenth century, or Farr's detailed analysis of household size in a number of districts in England and Wales in 1851.[36] There are no satisfactory general indexes to the censuses. Hence it is only by careful scrutiny of each census that the full scope of the material can be seen.

Limitations

In the earlier discussion there were references to some censuses as being more 'effective' than others. The term 'effective' may have several

34   The questions on fertility in the 1911 censuses were addressed to currently married women enumerated with their husbands. The restriction to 'currently married' excluded women whose marriages were unbroken during the childbearing period but whose husbands had died subsequently. Given the high level of mortality in the nineteenth century and the higher mortality of men than of women, this restriction means that the older the married women the smaller the proportion of those who were alive in 1911 and whose marriages had continued throughout the childbearing period, that would be included in the fertility study. The possible resultant bias in the apparent trend of fertility has thus to be taken into account. Modern fertility censuses by contrast, tend to enumerate all ever-married women. They are then classified and separate tabulations are undertaken for each category — e.g. for women whose marriages were unbroken during the reproductive period, for women married more than once, etc.

35   [L. M. Feery], *Census Reports of Great Britain*

36   1851 Census, *Population Tables I*, Vol. I (London, 1852) pp. xl-xliii and pp. xcix-ciii. See also the discussion in A. Block, *Estimating Housing Needs* (London, 1946) p. 32.

different implications. To cite a few examples, there is first of all the question of whether a particular census was actually completed. The abortive Irish census of 1813-15 was not completed; it was abandoned. In a much smaller degree the 1801 Census of Great Britain was also not complete. Writing in 1802 about the results of that census, John Rickman concluded that 'the total population of Great Britain must exceed the number of persons specified in the above summary, in as much as there are some parishes from which no returns have been received'. And it was widely believed that the 1801 figures were too low. John Heysham, who had supplied the statistics with which Joshua Milne had constructed the Carlisle life table, considered the 1801 enumeration in Carlisle to be poor, but the 1811 enumeration to be reasonably good, and there had probably been some improvement.

But even a census which completes its various procedures and appears to have enumerated the whole population, may not have achieved complete coverage. Of course, it is unlikely that any census would succeed in enumerating everyone. There is usually some undercounting, though there may also be some double counting if, for example, there are political or religious reasons for exaggerating the numbers of particular categories of people, or if enumerators are paid 'per head' of the population, or if the census is a *de facto* one and there is a long interval between the beginning and the end of the enumeration. The censuses of Britain and Ireland were taken on a *de facto* basis, recording the population present.[37] But the early censuses had their work spread over a period. And though a particular day was specified as census day, it is not clear whether the statistics relate exclusively to the persons who were present in the household on that given day. From 1841 onwards the position is much clearer, for the censuses specified the persons to be counted as those present on a particular night or, subsequently, returning home the following morning. It is necessary to look at the instructions on the schedules to see how the relevant population was defined, but this is equally important in respect of the various questions covered by the census, for the statistics may have been affected by the precise wording of the questions.

A reasonably comprehensive overall coverage does not exclude the possibility of significant omissions in respect of sub-groups of the population or of incomplete returns to particular questions in the schedule. An example of the latter type of omission occurred in connection with the voluntary question of age asked at the 1821 census. In a number of parishes the question was apparently not asked, for there were no returns at all for such parishes. Overall information on age was

---

37 From 1851 to 1871 the Irish censuses listed the normal members of a household who were absent on census night.

reported for about 88 per cent of the total population, and in using the age data it is clearly desirable to consider how far they were distorted as a result of the omissions. The former type of omission may be illustrated by the persistent under-enumeration of infants and young children. This is a well-known phenomenon, and the assessment of the error is complicated by the fact that there are also usually age-transfers – that is, some infants are reported as being one year old, and some one but less than two years of age are reported as two-year-olds. Farr believed that age transfers of this kind were a sufficient explanation of the apparent undercount, but not all of his contemporaries agreed.[38] And later studies showed that both omissions and age-transfers were involved.[39] Some types of omission may be caused by inadequate briefing of the enumerators or incomplete instructions in the schedule. A relevant example concerns household size, and the frequency of households containing various numbers of persons. The difficulty here concerns the way in which the concept of a household is applied or interpreted. A household is usually defined as consisting of those individuals who share a common board; lodgers who provide their own meals should thus be treated as separate households. But this is not always done by the enumerators and Farr drew attention to the consequent under-enumeration of single-person households in commenting on the results of the special analysis of households in fourteen sub-districts at the 1851 Census. The total number of households was thus too small and the average size of the household too large, and errors of this kind continued for a long period to affect estimates of housing needs. Errors of this kind still occur today, when the possibility of confusing boarders and lodgers is well known. The post-enumeration survey found some errors in the 1966 sample census of England and Wales: when corrected, the total number of households was increased by 1.4 per cent and the number of one-person households by about 7 per cent.[40]

In addition to various types of omissions, there are also positive errors

38   See W. L. Sargant 'Inconsistencies of the English census of 1861, with the Registrar-General's Reports: and deficiencies in the local registry of births', *J.R.S.S.*, Vol. 28,1865, pp. 73-110; and W. Farr 'On infant mortality, and on alleged inaccuracies of the census', *J.R.S.S.*, Vol. 28, 1865, pp. 125-149.

39   For a discussion of some of these studies see my paper, 'A note on the under-registration of births in Britain in the nineteenth century', *Population Studies*, Vol. 5, 1951-52 (November 1951). At the 1931 Census of England and Wales, some improvement in the reporting of infants was obtained by specifying that those who had not yet been named 'should be entered and described as "Baby".' Improvements in response are not infrequently achieved by better schedule design and more explicit briefing of enumerators and supervisors, as well as by the use of pilot surveys to test alternative schedules.

40   P. Gray and F. A. Gee, *A Quality Check on the 1966 Ten Per Cent Sample Census of England and Wales* (London, 1973) pp. 32-35.

— mis-statements arising out of ignorance or made consciously. Coming within the latter category would be wrong descriptions of marital condition: a couple living together but not married, might have described themselves as married, being unwilling to let the enumerator know the true situation. Similarly, a divorcee might describe herself as a widow — though there were very few divorces during the nineteenth century. Occupation also offers the possibility of conscious error, if the householder or some other member of the household wishes to report a higher social status than he actually has. Poorly-formulated questions on occupation increase this possibility. If the term 'engineer' is allowed as a description, it can cover a range of possible skills and socio-economic statuses, and so can the terms 'secretary', or 'farmer'. Some kinds of questions invite wrong answers, since they involve a high probability of memory error. This is the case with retrospective questions on births and deaths, especially when the time classification is specific — for example, when the events have to be reported by calendar year of occurrence. Even if the total number of events is correct — and it may well not be so — the distribution by calendar years may be wrong. It is understandable that the Irish censuses of 1841 to 1871 should have collected statistics of deaths, but it is clear that the statistics have to be treated with caution and assessed by the kinds of techniques used in evaluating retrospective surveys undertaken in developing societies today.[41] Questions on infirmities may also invite wrong

41 At the 1841 Census of Ireland, estimates of births by calendar year for the previous ten years were made by adding to the numbers alive at the relevant ages the numbers reported to have died at the corresponding ages during each year. It was believed that the numbers would be a 'near approximation' to the truth, though admittedly they could not take into account the vital events of families which have emigrated or had died out. The Report adds modestly: 'The mode in which these tables have been obtained, of course prevented our attempting to give more than the total in the year. We are, therefore, wholly unable to follow the subject with the minuteness statistical science would desire, as to the influence of hours, seasons, and localities, and a variety of causes'. [1841 Census of Ireland, *Report of the Commissioners* (Dublin, 1843) pp. xi and 458-459.]

An experiment carried out in North Carolina in 1965 indicates the magnitude of the errors arising in a retrospective survey covering only a relatively short period of time. Interviewers collected reports of births and deaths during the past year or past ten months from about 3,000 households in which the actual events were known from the registration records. Retrospective questioning yielded 92 per cent of the registered births and 82 per cent of the registered deaths, and infant deaths were especially poorly reported — only 53 per cent of the registered deaths. Since infant deaths must have constituted a large proportion of all deaths in Ireland in the 1830s, it is possible that the statistics collected at the 1841 Census represent a very serious understatement of general mortality. See E. S. Marks, W. Selzer and K. J. Krotki, *Population Growth Estimation: a Handbook of Vital Statistics Measurement*, New York, 1972 (unpublished), ch. 2. Details of the survey are given in D. G. Horwitz, 'Problems in designing interview surveys to measure population growth', *Proceedings of the Social Statistics Section, 1966,* American Statistical Association.

answers, especially if the conditions to be reported are regarded by the community as carrying a stigma.

Statistics of age are typically subject to error. Unless the question is unequivocal — as it was from 1851 onwards, namely age at last birthday — some respondents may round up their ages and others round them downwards. Much more serious errors may arise from the fact that, when birth registration is incomplete and when there is little need to use birth certificates, some people may have only a rough idea of their ages.[42] At the bottom end of the scale, parents may inflate the ages of their young children. At the other end of the age scale, old people who do not actually know how old they are may exaggerate them, so that they appear to have the distinction of 'great age'. Some nineteenth-century censuses undertook special surveys of people who had been reported as centenarians and found a good deal of overstatement of age among them.[43] With improved birth registration and the spread of literacy, later censuses tended to show proportionately fewer centenarians — an indication of improvement in accuracy and not of a rise in mortality. Nowadays, with virtually complete birth registration and with the need to provide evidence of age on a variety of occasions — not least in connection with social security benefits — there is a much higher degree of accuracy. Even so, some of the earlier patterns of error remain — such as the rounding of ages and, in some cases, the understatement of women's ages.[44]

42   There is a discussion of errors in the 1851 returns in 1851 Census of Great Britain, *Population Tables, II,* Vol. 1 (London, 1854) pp. xxiii-xxv.

43   For example, in France the 1861 Census reported 256 centenarians, but only 127 were reported in 1866, 190 in 1872 and 194 in 1886. An official inquiry undertaken in connection with the 1886 Census showed that of the 194 reported centenarians, no documentation was available in respect of forty-eight. Of the remaining 146, sixty-three were definitely not centenarians but mainly octogenarians, leaving only eighty-three, sixteen of whom were able to produce their baptismal records, while the others had other documents or statements which had been made by their parents. See E. Levasseur, *La Population Francaise,* Vol. 2 (Paris, 1891) pp. 326-332. The 1871 Census of England and Wales reported 160 centenarians out of a total population of 22.712 millions; that of Ireland reported 983 out of a total population of 5.412 millions.

44   The 1961 post-enumeration survey asked for both date of birth and age in years at last birthday and completed months since then. When the answers were checked against birth certificates, the former question was found to yield more accurate answers than the latter. As a result, the 1966 Census of England and Wales asked for date of birth instead of age. A further check was carried out by the 1966 post-enumeration survey. Out of a sample of 2,650 cases, there was complete agreement with the birth certificate in 2,417 cases, or 91.2 per cent, plus a further sixty-three cases (2.4 per cent) in which there was disagreement only in respect of the day of birth, and not the month or year (P. Gray and F. A. Gee, *A Quality Check on the . . . Sample Census,* pp. 107-109).

Possibilities for Re-analysis

The discussion of census errors did not aim to frighten potential users of the censuses, but to draw their attention to the need for a careful assessment of the quality of the data they wish to use. Assessment can be undertaken at different levels, depending upon the kind of data involved and the existence of independent checks. When a local study is based upon the enumerators' books for the 1851 or 1861 censuses, assessment may be possible at the level of the individual or of the household, by checking against parish registers or against the records of civil vital registration. Local sources other than the parish registers may also supply relevant information.[45] Detailed comparisons of this kind are time-consuming and unlikely to be undertaken unless they are important in studying local communities. At the national level, direct tests are far more difficult, though it would not be out of the question to compare, say, the age entries for a properly designed sample from the enumerators' books with the corresponding birth certificates, and some work on these lines has been done by Razzell in connection with his studies of the parish registers.[46] Such direct tests are not possible in using the published census statistics, which necessarily hide the identity of individuals. But other kinds of tests may be possible. If there are comprehensive registers for various professions, it may be useful to compare the numbers with those in the census, in order to see if there has been a gross inflation of occupational status in the census.[47] Vital statistics may help in trying to see whether there was serious under-reporting of divorced persons who, when divorce was considered reprehensible, might have described themselves as widows or widowers. For age errors there are very many useful tests, generally described in textbooks on demographic analysis, and some techniques which can be used both to test and to reduce age mis-statements.[48]

45   A valuable discussion of inaccuracies at the local level, as revealed by the examination of enumerators' books for the 1851 and 1861 censuses of England and Wales, will be found in P. M. Tillott, 'Sources of inaccuracy in the 1851 and 1861 censuses', in E. A. Wrigley, ed., *Nineteenth-century Society*.

46   P. E. Razzell, *op. cit.*

47   There were not infrequent claims that the numbers of people employed in particular categories of occupations were greatly understated. For example, in the debate on the 1870 Census Bill, Mr. M. T. Bass attacked the census, saying that 'he had it, on good authority, that there was scarcely any return of occupations in the Census which was not as defective as that of landowners which was mentioned the other night'. He instanced the case of brewers. In the 1861 Census, the number of brewers and their workmen was given as 20,300. But a Revenue return gave the numbers as over 33,000, excluding workmen. *Hansard*, 3rd. series, 203 (1870), Col. 1002.

48   On these techniques, see, for example, N. Carrier and J. Hobcraft, *Demographic Estimation for Developing Societies* (London, 1971).

Problems of comparability also have to be dealt with when more than one census is used. Boundaries are revised, and local government units are changed.[49] Changes in the listing and classification of occupations present some of the most difficult problems of comparability. Nevertheless even those difficulties can be met to a reasonable extent, as may be seen from the work of Bowley and the recent, detailed classifications produced by Armstrong.[50] The censuses are prime documents in studying nineteenth-century social and economic history. Treated with the help of methods of analysis and correction now available and assessed against a background of more than 150 years of experience, nineteenth-century census data are likely to be even more illuminating today than they were to those who took part in producing them.

49   These changes are particularly important in studying the history of urban development in Britain. For a valuable analysis of the growth of urban populations in Britain in the nineteenth century, see the evidence of the Registrars General to the pre-war Barlow Commission (the Royal Commission on the Distribution of the Industrial Population which reported in 1940), unpublished but available in the library of the General Register Office.

50   Bowley was concerned with an attempt to estimate the changing size of the 'middle class' and 'working class' populations. See A. L. Bowley, *Wages and Income in the United Kingdom since 1860* (Cambridge, 1937), pp. 127-136.

For W. A. Armstrong's detailed classification of the nineteenth-century census data on occupation, see his chapter, 'The use of information about occupation', in E. A. Wrigley, ed., *Nineteenth-century Society*.

Appendix 1

Great Britain: Census Acts and Census Dates, 1801-1891

Census	Act	Date of Act	Date of Census
1801	41 Geo. III. c. 15	31 December 1800	10 March 1801
1811	51 Geo. III. c. 6	22 March 1811	27 May 1811
1821	1 Geo. IV. c. 94	24 July 1820	28 May 1821
1831	11 Geo. IV & 1 Will. IV. c. 30	23 June 1830	30 May 1831
1841	3 & 4 Vict. c. 99	10 August 1840	
	4 & 5 Vict. c. 7	6 April 1841	6 June 1841
1851	13 & 14 Vict. c. 53	5 August 1840	30 March 1851
1861	England & Wales:		
	23 & 24 Vict. c. 61	6 August 1860	7 April 1861
	Scotland:		
	23 & 24 Vict. c. 98	20 August 1860	7 April 1861
1871	England & Wales:		
	33 & 34 Vict. c. 107	10 August 1870	2 April 1871
	Scotland:		
	33 & 34 Vict. c. 108	10 August 1870	2 April 1871
1881	England & Wales:		
	43 & 44 Vict. c. 37	7 September 1880	3 April 1881
	Scotland:		
	43 & 44 Vict. c. 38	7 September 1880	3 April 1881
1891	England & Wales:		
	53 & 54 Vict. c. 61	18 August 1890	5 April 1891
	Scotland:		
	53 & 54 Vict. c. 38	14 August 1890	5 April 1891

Appendix 2

Ireland: Census Acts and Census Dates, 1821-1891

Census	Act	Date of Act	Date of Census
1821	55 Geo. III. c. 120	28 June 1815	28 May 1821
	3 Geo. IV. c. 5	11 March 1822	
1831	1 Will. IV. c. 19	30 March 1831	*
1841	3 & 4 Vict. c. 100	10 August 1840	Sunday 6 June 1841
	4 & 5 Vict. c. 7	6 April 1841	
1851	13 & 14 Vict. c. 44	29 July 1850	Sunday 30 March 1851
1861	23 & 24 Vict. c. 62	6 August 1860	Sunday 7 April 1861
1871	33 & 34 Vict. c. 80	9 August 1870	Sunday 2 April 1871
1881	43 & 44 Vict. c. 28	26 August 1880	Sunday 3 April 1881
1891	53 & 54 Vict. c. 46	18 August 1890	Sunday 5 April 1891

* The Census Act did not specify a date or list the questions to be covered. Nor is this information given in the census report. Advertisements in the Irish press suggest that 31 May 1831 was the date to which 'normal residence' was to be referred. But in some counties enumerators were not appointed until then, while in County Kerry they were appointed 2 June. In County Clare an adjourned meeting was advertised to be held on 28 June, at which time books, schedules, forms and instructions would be distributed to the enumerators.

Appendix 3

List of published Census Reports

Census		BPP	Order Paper ( ) or Command [ ] No.	Report
1801	1801	6	(140)	Initial Abstract
	1801-02	6	(9)	Parish Register Abstract. Observations.
	1801-02	7	(112)	Enumeration Abstract. Pt. I, E. & W. Pt. II, Scotland.
1811	1812	10	(12)	Comparative Statement, 1801, 1811.
	1812	11	(316)	Preliminary Observations. Enumeration Abstract.
			(317)	Parish Register Abstract.
1821	1822	15	(502)	Preliminary Observations. Enumeration & Parish Register Abstract.
	1822	21	(8)	Comparative Statement, 1801-21.
1831	1831	18	(348)	* Comparative Account, 1801-31.
	1833	36	(149)	Enumeration Abstract. Vol. I, Bedford to Somerset.
	1833	37		* Enumeration Abstract. Vol. II, Southampton to York, Wales, Scotland. Index.
	1833	38		Parish Register Abstract.
1841	1841 Sess. 2	2	(52)	* Comparative Statement, 1801-41, etc.
	1843	22	(496)	* Enumeration Abstract. Pt. I, E. & W.
			(511)	* Index, E. & W.
			(498)	* Enumeration Abstract. Pt. II, Scotland.
			(506)	* Index. Scotland.
	1843	23	(497)	* Age Abstract. Pt. I, E. & W. Pt. II, Scotland.
	1844	27	(587)	* Occupation Abstract. Pt. I, E. & W.
			(588)	* Occupation Abstract. Pt. II, Scotland.
	1845	25	(623)	Parish Register Abstract.
1851	1851	43	[1339]	* Census Forms & Instructions.
			[1399]	* Preliminary Tables.
	1852-53	85	[1631]	* Population Tables I, Vol. I, E. & W. Divisions I-IV.
	1852-53	86	[1632]	* Population Tables I, Vol. II, Divisions VII-XI. Scotland. Islands.
	1852-53	87	[1633]	Index.
	1852-53	88-I	[1691-I]	* Population Tables II, Vol. I: Age, Marriage, Occupation, Birth-place, etc., E. & W. Divisions I-VI.

	Year	Session	Paper No.		Title
	1852-53	88-II	[1691-II]	*	Population Tables II, Vol. II, Ditto. Divisions VII-XI. Scotland. Islands.
	1852-53	89	[1690]	*	Religious Worship. E. & W.
	1852-53	90	[1692]	*	Education. E. & W.
1861	1854	59	[1764]	*	Religious Worship & Education. Scotland.
	1861	50	[2846]		E. & W. Preliminary Report.
			[2870]		Scotland Preliminary Report.
	1862	50	[3056]		E. & W. Vol. I, Population Tables. Index.
			[3013]		Scotland Vol. I, Population Tables. Report.
	1863	53-1	[3221]	*	E. & W. Vol. III, General Report.
		53-2	{	*	E. & W. Vol. II, Age, Marriage, Occupation, Birth-place. Divisions I-III.
					E. & W. Vol. II, Age, Marriage, Occupation, Birth-place. Divisions IV-XI. Islands.
1871	1864	51	[3275]	*	Scotland. Vol. II, Age, Marriage, Occupation, Birth-place. Report. Index.
	1871	59	[381]	*	E. & W. Preliminary Report.
			[380]	*	Scotland Preliminary Report.
	1872	66-1	[676]	*	E. & W. Vol. I, Population. Ancient Counties.
	1872	66-2	[676-I]	*	E. & W. Vol. II, Population. Registration Counties.
			[676-II]	*	E. & W. Index.
	1872	68	[592]	*	Scotland. Vol. I, Population. Report.
	1873	71-1	[872]	*	E. & W. Vol. III, Age, Marriage, Occupation, Birth-place.
	1873	71-2	[872-I]	*	E. & W. Vol. IV, General Report.
	1873	73	[841]	*	Scotland. Vol. II, Age, Education, Marriage, Birth-place, Occupation, Births, Marriages & Deaths. 1861-70 Report. Index.
1881	1881	96	[2955]	*	E. & W. Preliminary Report.
			[2957]		Scotland Preliminary Report.
	1882	76	[3320]	*	Scotland Vol. I, Population. Report.
	1883	78	[3562]	*	E. & W. Vol. I, Population. Ancient Counties.
	1883	79	[3563]	*	E. & W. Vol. II, Population. Registration Counties.
	1883	80	[3722]	*	E. & W. Vol. III, Age, Marriage, Occupation, Birth-place.
			[3797]		E. & W. Vol. IV, General Report.
			[3643]	*	E. & W. Islands in the British Sea.
	1883	81	[3657]		Scotland Vol. II, Age, Education, Marriage, Birth-place, Occupation. Report. Index.

Appendix 3—cont.

Census	BPP		Order Paper ( ) or Command [ ] No.	Report
1891	1890-01	94	{[6422] / [6390]}	* E. & W. Preliminary Report. / * Scotland. Preliminary Report.
	1892	94	[6755]	* Scotland. Vol. I, Population. Report.
	1893-94	104	{[6948] / [7216]}	* E. & W. Vol. I, Population. Counties. / * E. & W. Index.
	1893-94	105	[6948-I]	* E. & W. Vol. II, Population, Registration Areas and Sanitary Districts.
	1893-94	106	{[7058] / [7222]}	* E. & W. Vol. III, Age, Marriage, Occupation, Birth-place. / * E. & W. Vol. IV, General Report.
	1893-94	107	{[7133] / [6936]}	* E. & W. Islands in the British Sea. / * Scotland. Vol. I, Supplement. Boundary Changes.
	1893-94	108	{[6937] / [7134]}	* Scotland. Vol. II, Pt. I, Age, Education, Marriage, Birth-place, Report. / * Scotland. Vol. II, Pt. II, Occupation. Report. Index.

* Included in Irish University Press series, **Population** (25 vols.)

Appendix 4

Census Reports for Ireland, 1821-1891, in Parliamentary Papers

Census		BPP	Order Paper ( ) or Command [ ] No.		Report
1821	1822	14	(36)		Initial Abstract, comparing 1813.
	1824	22	(577)		Enumeration Abstract, comparing 1813.
1831	1833	39	(634)		Enumeration Abstract.
			(254)		County Summary.
			(23)		Comparative Abstract, 1821-31.
1841	1843	24	(504)	*	Report.
	1843	51	(459)		Enumeration Abstract.
			(354)		Population of Ireland & Scotland. Ireland – Religion 1834.
1851	1851	50	[1400]		Comparative Abstract, 1841-51.
	1852	46	[673]		County Abstract, 1841-51.
			[373]		Union & Electoral Division Abstract, 1841-51.
	1852-53	91	[various]		Pt. I, Population. Separate counties of Leinster.
	1852-53	91	[various]	*	Pt. I, Population. Vol. I, Leinster.
			[various]	*	Pt. I, Population. Vol. II, Munster.
	1852-53	92	[various]	*	Pt. I, Population. Vol. III, Ulster.
			[various]	*	Pt. I, Population. Vol. IV, Connaught.
	1852-53	93	[1589]		Pt. II, Agricultural Returns.
	1854	58	[1765]		Pt. III, Disease.
	1856	29	[2053]		Pt. IV, Age. Education.
	1856	30	[2087-I]		Pt. V, Deaths: Vol. I, Report.
	1856	31	[2087-II]		Pt. V, Deaths: Vol. II, Tables.
	1862	51	[2134]		Pt. VI, General Report. Index.
	1862	51	[2942]	*	Index.
1861	1861	50	[2865]		Preliminary & Comparative Abstracts, 1841-61.
	1863	54	[3204]		Pt. I, Population. Vol. I, Leinster.
					Pt. I, Population. Vol. II, Munster.
	1863	55			Pt. I, Population. Vol. III, Ulster.
					Pt. I, Population. Vol. IV, Connaught & Summary.

Appendix 4—cont.

Census		BPP	Order Paper ( ) or Command [ ] No.	Report
	1863	56	[3204-I]	Pt. II, Age. Education. Vol. I.
	1863	57		Pt. II, Age. Education. Vol. II.
	1863	58	[3204-II]	Pt. III, Vital Statistics. Vol. I, Disease.
				Pt. III, Vital Statistics. Vol. II, Deaths.
	1863	59	[3204-III]	Pt. IV, Religion, Education, Occupation. Vol. I.
	1863	60		Pt. IV, Religion, Education, Occupation. Vol. II.
	1863	61	[3204-IV]	General Report. Index.
1871	1871	59	[375]	Preliminary & Comparative Abstracts, 1841-71.
	1872	67	[662]	Pt. I, Population. Age, etc. Vol. I, Leinster.
	1873	72-I	[873 I-IV]	Pt. I, Population. Age, etc. Vol. II, Munster, Clare to Limerick.
	1873	72-II	[873 V-VII]	Pt. I, Population. Age, etc. Vol. II, Munster, Tipperary, Waterford.
			[876]	Pt. II, Vital Statistics. Vol. I, Disease.
	1874	74-I	[964]	Pt. I, Population. Age, etc. Vol. III, Ulster.
	1874	74-II	[1106]	Pt. I, Population. Age, etc. Vol. IV, Connaught. Summary.
	1874	74-III	[1000]	Pt. II, Vital Statistics. Vol. II, Deaths.
	1876	81	[1377]	Pt. III, General Report.
	1877	87	[1711]	Index.
1881	1881	96	[2931]	Preliminary Report.
	1881	97	[3042]	Population. Age, etc. Leinster.
	1882	76	[3365]	General Report.
	1882	77	[3148]	Population. Age, etc. Munster.
	1882	78	[3204]	Population. Age, etc. Ulster.
	1882	79	[3268]	Population. Age, etc. Connaught.
			[3379]	Index (supplement).
1891	1890-91	94	[6379]	Preliminary Report.
	1890-91	95	[6515]	Pt. I, Population. Age, etc. Vol. I, Leinster.
	1892	90	[6780]	Pt. II, General Report.
			[6781]	Index (supplement).
	1892	91	[6567]	Pt. I, Population. Age, etc. Vol. II, Munster.
	1892	92	[6626]	Pt. I, Population. Age, etc. Vol. III, Ulster.
	1892	93	[6685]	Pt. I, Population. Age, etc. Vol. IV, Connaught.

* Included in the Irish University Press series, **Population** (25 vols.)

The Documents

Population 1
Comparative account of the population of Great Britain in the years 1801, 1811, 1821, 1831 (428 pp. 2 coloured maps)

This is a summary of the findings of the first four census reports. Tables of returns for the parishes and townships of England, Wales and Scotland are present in alphabetical order. In addition to the population figures from the censuses, the tables include a column showing the 'annual value of real property in 1815' based on the Poor Rate Return compiled from property tax assessments. The percentage increase in population is given for each country in the three decennial periods. Prefixed are the questions addressed to the overseers in England and schoolmasters in Scotland, who conducted the census before the household schedule was introduced in 1840. The section on Wales is prefaced by a brief description of the formation of the border counties during the reign of Henry VIII and a glossary of place names.

Besides arranging the abstracts of the returns, John Rickman (1771-1840) contributed 'a statement of progress in the inquiry regarding the occupation of families and persons and the duration of life'. In this report Rickman, who directed the first four censuses, comments on the defects of the previous censuses and on preliminary findings of the 1831 census. Figures for the major towns show the dramatic increase which had taken place in the urban population (and the need which had arisen for parliamentary reform). The 'statement' also includes an interesting account of the history of metropolitan London, with a map illustrating the parish boundaries. Another feature is an analysis of the population of Essex made by Rickman. His sources for the origins of place names, and historical anecdotage range from Tacitus to Norse war songs and Saxon chronicles. He describes the 'increased duration of life in England' as phenomenal: he believed that mortality rates had decreased from one person in every thirty-seven of the population for the greater part of the eighteenth century, to one in sixty for the 1810-20 period.

Original reference
1831   [348] XVIII   Comparative account of population.

Population 2
Report from the commissioners appointed to take the census of Ireland for the Year 1841. (896 pp. 5 maps, 1 folding coloured; 3 charts, 2 folding)

'The 1841 census is probably the first with a really high degree of accuracy', writes a prominent Irish historian. It provides a unique record of social and economic conditions at a watershed in history: underlining the state of pre-famine Ireland and making possible an assessment of the changes wrought by 'the great hunger'.

The commissioners achieved such satisfactory results partly because they were able to profit by the experience gained at previous censuses and partly because of their zeal in following a 'strict mode of enquiry': they had the returns made by a 'highly disciplined body of men' (the constabulary), on the same day throughout the country and they applied a 'method of verification'.

Not merely a 'bare enumeration' of the population, this remarkable census was also a social survey. It contains detailed information on the composition of households; abstracts on age, education, marriage, housing and occupations. The tables and charts provide the basis for accepted views about the pattern of Irish society and remain an inexhaustible source for fresh interpretation.

The volume includes a report of the commissioners with an appendix, county tables (which are broken down into baronies, parishes and towns), a summary and miscellaneous tables under such headings as emigration and rural economy. It also has the report on tables of deaths by Surgeon W. R. Wilde, father of Oscar Wilde, that reflects the author's wide learning along with his medical skill (an interesting feature is the Irish form of disease names given in the report).

One of the commissioners, Sir Thomas Larcom (1801-79) had organized the extremely valuable work done on the ordnance survey. He was responsible for the systematic classification of the occupations and general condition of the people taken for the first time at the 1841 census. His biographer in the *Dictionary of National Biography* claims that 'England afterwards adopted the general plan of the Irish census'.

Original reference
1843   [504] XXIV   1841 census, Ireland, rep. of commissioners, appendix
                           and index.

Population 3-5

1841 Census Great Britain

The method initiated for conducting the census in 1841 has stood the test of time and has not been substantially altered since that time. Responsibility for carrying out the official numbering of the population passed to the newly-established General Register Office. The household schedule was introduced with a penalty imposed for failure to complete it on a certain date. Sunday became census day.

The 1841 census was planned with a thoroughness that had characterized the civil registration of births, marriages and deaths in England and Wales. For the purpose of the census each of the 2,193 registration districts was sub-divided into areas that could be covered by enumerators in one day. Each parish in Scotland was similarly divided; here civil registration was not established until 1855 and superintendence of the census was again entrusted to the official schoolmaster or other suitable person.

In addition to name, sex, age and occupation, householders were asked to state the birthplace and nationality of all persons sleeping in the house on 6 June 1841. The occupations of the people (IUP volume 5) are listed alphabetically under counties and large towns and the exact employment of every person, distinguishing those under and those over twenty years of age, was stated. The ages of the parish population are shown for the two groups (under twenty, twenty and above) in the Enumeration Abstract (IUP volume 3). In the Age Abstract (IUP volume 4) the ages of the entire population are given under counties, hundreds and large towns in quinquennial age groups and, in an appendix, the children in every county are shown at each year of age to fifteen. Indexes to every parish and place appear at the end of these two abstracts.

A comparison with the results of previous censuses is made in the preface to the Occupation Abstract, which also contains analyses of the numbers employed in the mining and manufacturing industries, along with detailed information as to how inmates of institutions were employed. Rickman's calculations on the population of England and Wales, 1570-1750, are printed in the preface to the Enumeration Abstract, the appendix of which gives the population of parliamentary cities and boroughs formed under the 1832 Reform Act. An explanation is provided of the distinction made between the 'ancient' (historic) boundaries and the registration counties.

Volume 3   1841 Census Great Britain: statements on population, enumeration abstract, indexes to place names. (760 pp.)

Original references

1841	[52] II Sess. 2	Statements on population.
1843	[496] XXII	Enumeration abstract, part I England and Wales.
	[511]	Index, England and Wales.
	[498]	Enumeration abstract, part II Scotland.
	[506]	Index, Scotland.

Volume 4 1841 Census Great Britain: age abstract, with appendices. (664 pp.)

Original reference
1843   [497] XXIII   Age abstract.

Volume 5 1841 Census Great Britain: occupation abstract, with preface. (480 pp. 2 folding tables)

Original references
1844   [587] XXVII   Occupation abstract, England and Wales.
        [588]   Occupation abstract, Scotland.

Population 6-11
1851 Census Great Britain

This saw the first systematic attempt to classify occupations. Both the scope and coverage of the census were greatly extended. The householder's schedule required for each person a statement of relationship to the head of the household, of marital condition (i.e. unmarried, widow, etc.) and whether the person was blind or deaf and dumb. Exact age was also asked for the first time. Provision was made to enumerate all persons on board vessels lying in harbour and on British ships at sea, in the army abroad, Europeans serving with the East India Company and British subjects residing in various foreign states.

A fundamental change took place in the form of presentation. The Registrar-General had grouped the registration counties of England and Wales into eleven registration divisions. Census statistics for each parish or place were arranged according to their respective registration districts and sub-districts and grouped according to their respective registration divisions. Scotland was divided into two groups of counties, and islands in the British seas formed a fourteenth group. Population Tables I (IUP volumes 6 and 7) give the acreage, details of housing 1841-51 and the population, male and female, as enumerated at each census from 1801. Comments on significant movements of people revealed are appended. Population Tables II (IUP volumes 8 and 9) contain abstracts for 1851 only, of the ages, civil condition, occupations and birthplaces of the people, together with statistics of the blind, deaf and dumb, and of the inmates of workhouses, prisons, lunatic asylums and hospitals.

Each series is prefaced by a report and summary tables. The reports have been described as 'the most interesting in the census series from 1801 to 1931'. Signed by George Graham, the Registrar-General, and by William Farr and Horace Mann, they provide considerable insight into contemporary social thought and attitudes. Each report is illustrated by maps, charts and appendices. Particularly noteworthy are the maps showing density of population and distribution according to occupation.

Two important features of the 1851 census were the inquiries into religion and education. Because of opposition raised to making the answering of questions on these subjects binding, the census commissioners were obliged to conduct the surveys on a voluntary basis. However, there were few refusals to participate. Hence this census of Britain taken at the middle of the nineteenth century. was the first to contain data on education and the only one which included information on religious attendance.

Volume 6 1851 Census Great Britain: instructions to enumerators, tables of population and housing, numbers of inhabitants 1801-51, volume I with census report. (936 pp. 12 folding maps, 8 coloured)

Original references
1851   [1339] XLIII   Instructions to enumerators.
       [1399]   Tables of population and housing.
1852-53 [1631] LXXXV   Numbers of inhabitants, vol. I.

Volume 7 1851 Census Great Britain: numbers of inhabitants 1801-51, volume II, index to place names. (454 pp. 5 folding tables)

Original references
1852-53 [1632] LXXXVI Numbers of inhabitants, vol. II.
1852-53 [1633] LXXXVII Index.

Volume 8 1851 Census Great Britain: ages, civil condition, occupations and birthplaces, volume I. (912 pp. 1 folding coloured map)

Original reference
1852-53 [1691-I] LXXXVIII   Ages, civil condition, occupations, birthplaces,
Pt. I   vol. I.

Volume 9 1851 Census Great Britain: ages, civil condition, occupations and birthplaces, volume II, with index. (576 pp.)

Original reference
1852-53 [1691-II] LXXXVIII Pt. II   Ages, civil condition, occupations, birthplaces,
                           vol. II.

Volume 10   1851 Census Great Britain: report and tables on religious worship, England and Wales. (456 pp.)

Original reference
1852-53 [1690] LXXXIX Religious worship, England and Wales.

Volume 11   1851 Census Great Britain: reports and tables on education, England and Wales, and on religious worship and education, Scotland. (620 pp. 4 tables, 2 coloured)

Original references
1852-53 [1692] XC   Education, England and Wales.
1854   [1764] LIX   Religious worship, education, Scotland.

Population 12-14

1851 Census Ireland

The IUP selection from the six-part 1851 Irish census contains the vital information on population in the strict demographic sense, together with the invaluable General Report. In their preliminary report, the chief commissioner, Registrar-General William Donnelly and William R. Wilde, his assistant, paid tribute to the constabulary who continued to act as enumerators in Ireland.

IUP volumes 13 and 14 (Part I) comprise tables for counties and baronies, subdivided into parishes, townlands and towns giving area, population and number of houses in 1841 and 1851, and Poor Law valuation in 1851. In addition each county abstract contains a statistical breakdown according to Poor Law unions and electoral divisions. For each county there are summary tables according to baronies and unions.

The General Report is accompanied by an appendix, county tables, miscellaneous tables and an index to place names. This volume summarizes the findings of the monumental census of 1851, which took five years to complete. It is particularly useful for information on emigration and the number of Irish speakers.

The 1851 census of Ireland records the profound changes in the population structure caused by the ravages of the Great Famine. IUP volumes 2 (1841 census), 12, 13 and 14 document the most significant decennial period in modern Irish social history, and they are an important supplement to the Irish University Press Famine (Ireland) Set.

Volume 12   1851 Census Ireland: part I, Leinster and Munster: area, population and housing. (760 pp.)

Original references
1852-53 XCI Pt. I   [1465] [1553] [1481] [1486] [1488] [1492] [1503]
                           [1496] [1502] [1564] [1527] [1544] [1552] [1550]
                           [1551] [1543] [1554] [1549] [1545] [1546], vols. I
                           and II. Leinster and Munster: area, population and
                           housing.

Volume 13   1851 Census Ireland: part I, Ulster and Connacht: area, population and housing. (592 pp.)

Original references
1852-53 XCII Pt. I   [1565] [1547] [1563] [1567] [1570] [1574] [1571]
                           [1575] [1579] [1557] [1548] [1542] [1555] [1560],
                           vols. III and IV. Ulster and Connacht: area population
                           and housing.

Volume 14   1851 Census Ireland: part VI, general report. (832 pp.)

Original reference
1856   [2134] XXXI Pt. VI General report.

Volume 15 1861 and 1871 Censuses England and Wales: general reports. (732 pp.)

A valuable feature introduced in 1861, the General Reports provide critical commentary and summary tables of the complete census returns for England and Wales. Included in the 1861 Report are statements of baptisms and burials 1700-1840, of the estimated population 1701-91 and of the enumerated population estimated to the middle of census years 1801-61, and of the estimated population in 1651 and 1751. The section on laws regulating the growth of nations has a criticism of the Malthusian theory. A note on the area and population of the British empire is supported by tables, compiled from colonial census returns, given in the appendix. The latter also contains data on the number of farmers and farm-labourers and the size of holdings for ten counties only (the agricultural inquiry of 1851 was regarded as faulty).

The appendix to the 1861 Report concludes with two extremely interesting papers by William Farr. In the first he discussed the census of production, the etymology of names by which various occupations were known, the value to the community of the professional classes and the occupational classification which he had prepared for use in connection with the census of 1851. The second paper consists of a letter to the Registrar-General on a proposed inquiry into occupations, with an outline of the heads of inquiry, a sample reply on coal mining in Staffordshire, a brief memorandum on the Cornish mines and a draft report on the medical profession.

The General Report of 1871 contains, *inter alia,* comparisons with French demography and a description of territorial divisions in England, Wales, Scotland and Ireland.

Original references
1863   [3221] LIII Pt. I 1861 Census, England and Wales, General rep.
1873   [872-I] LXXI Pt. II   1871 Census, England and Wales, General rep.

Population 16-19
1871 Census England and Wales
1871 Census Scotland

From 1861, for census purposes, Scotland was separated from the rest of Great Britain and placed under the control of a Registrar-General for Scotland. In general the method of organization developed in London was adopted north of the border. Two questions were added to the Scottish census schedule: the number of rooms with one or more windows, and the number of children between the ages of five and fifteen who were attending school or being educated at home.

The questions asked at the census of 1871 only differed substantially from those of the preceding English and Scottish censuses by the inclusion of 'unemployed' in the occupations section. The infirmities inquiry was expanded to include deaf and dumb, blind, imbecile or idiot, and lunatic (not surprisingly for an age self-conscious about mental illnesses, the findings under these headings were described as 'very untrustworthy' by the 1890 Census Committee).

The value of the age and occupation tables was realized in the England and Wales census report.

A standard pattern emerged for the presentation of the Scottish census findings. Preliminary returns were followed by two volumes of population tables with comprehensive reports. The 1871 census of Scotland, volume I contains information on the population of various regional divisions, and on the number of houses. Volume II provides details of ages, education, civil condition (marital or non-marital status), birthplaces and occupations of the people. The form of the English and Welsh census report was changed in 1871. Volume I of the Population Tables contains details for 'ancient' or historic counties; Volume II analyses the returns according to registration or Poor Law union counties, and has an index to place names appended. Volume III, Population Abstracts, comprises the findings on ages, civil condition, occupations and birthplaces. The General Report has already been referred to (IUP volume 15).

1871 Census England and Wales

Volume 16 1871 Census England and Wales: preliminary report with tables, area, housing and population, volume I. (768 pp.)

Original references
1871   [C.381] LIX   Preliminary rep.
1872   [C.676] LXVI Pt. I   Area, housing, population, vol. I.

Volume 17 1871 Census England and Wales: area, housing and population volume II, index to population tables. (800 pp. 11 folding coloured maps)

Original references
1872   [C.676-I] LXVI Pt. II Area, housing, population, vol. II.
        [C.676-II]   1 Index.

Volume 18 1871 Census England and Wales: ages, civil condition, occupations and birthplaces. (752 pp.)

Original reference
1873   [C.872] LXXII Pt. I Ages, civil condition, occupations, birthplaces.

1871 Census Scotland

Volume 19 1871 Census Scotland: tables of population, eighth decennial census, volumes I and II, with reports. (1,208 pp.)

Original references
1871   [C.380] LIX   Tables, Scotland.
1872   [C.592] LXVIII Eighth census, vol. I.
1873   [C.841] LXXIII Eighth census, vol. II.

Population 20-25

1881 and 1891 Censuses England and Wales
1891 Census Scotland

The IUP Population Sct concludes with the 1881 General Report for England and Wales, and the complete findings of 1891 British census. In the 1881 General Report statistics of the Empire were compressed into a single summary table, while that of 1891 noted changes made in the occupational classification.

At the 1891 England and Wales census questions were asked on two new subjects: the extent to which Welsh was spoken in Wales and Monmouthshire, and the number of households with five rooms and under (information on Gaelic speakers had been sought in Scotland since the previous census).

An attempt was also made to distinguish employers from employees, but the schedule forms were filled in incorrectly. The introduction of this distinction led to a reduction in the number of separate occupational headings from 400 to 347. The method of presenting the occupation data remained the same as in 1851, that is in counties arranged divisionally.

The detailed age analysis introduced in 1851 was modified at each subsequent census. In 1871 for example, the age groups provided were quinquennial to twenty-five and decennial from twenty-five to seventy-five years and over, both for counties and the country as a whole. In 1891 the occupations of persons aged ten years and upwards were abstracted, age columns being provided for England and Wales quinquennially from ten to twenty-five years and for decennial periods to sixty-five, beyond which, as in 1881, there was one age group only.

The 1891 census of Scotland contained volume I with a supplement, volume II in two parts and appendices. The boundary changes under the Local Government (Scotland) Act, 1889 were incorporated in the tables, together with more precise information on the status of the Gaelic language.

1881 and 1891 Censuses England and Wales

Volume 20   1881 and 1891 Censuses England and Wales: 1881 general report; 1891 preliminary and general reports, population of islands. (504 pp.)

Original references
1883   [C.3797] LXXX   General rep.
1890-91 [C.6422] XCIV   Preliminary rep.
1893-94 [C.7222] CVI   General rep.
1893-94 [C.7133] CVII   Islands in the British seas.

1891 Census England and Wales

Volume 21 1891 Census England and Wales: area, housing and population volume I, index to the population tables. (752 pp.)

Original references
1893-94 [C.6948] CIV   Area, housing, population, vol. I.
         [C.7216]   Index.

Volume 22 1891 Census England and Wales: area, housing and population volume II. (1,216 pp. 11 folding coloured maps)

Original reference
1893-94 [C.6948-I] CV   Area, housing, population, vol. II.

Volume 23 1891 Census England and Wales: ages, marital condition, occupations, birthplaces and infirmities. (636 pp.)

Original reference
1893-94 [C.7058] CVI   Ages, marital condition, occupations, birthplaces, infirmities.

1891 Census Scotland

Volume 24 1891 Census Scotland: tables of population, tenth decennial census, volume I, supplement, volume II part I, with reports. (984 pp.)

Original references
1890-91 [C.6390] XCIV   Tables, Scotland.
1892   [C.6755] XCIV   Tenth census, vol. I.
1893-94 [C.6936] CVII   Supplement to vol. I.
         [C.6937]   Vol. II, part I.

Volume 25 1891 Census Scotland: tenth decennial census, volume II part II with report. (904 pp.)

Original reference
1893-94 [C.7134] CVIII   Vol. II, part II.

Bibliography

Censuses usually provide information on many aspects of a society. In a short bibliography it is not possible to do more than pick out a few aspects, and this is especially the case in dealing with the span of time and the range of subjects covered by the censuses of Great Britain and Ireland from 1801 to 1891. The references which follow represent no more than a tiny fraction of the writing on the various topics and the aim is simply to introduce the reader to some of the more useful publications, with the aid of which a detailed study can be pursued.

The censuses in general
A helpful discussion of the problems involved in collecting demographic data by census and other means will be found in H. Shryock, J. S. Siegel and Associates, *The Methods and Materials of Demography,* Vol. 1, chs. 2 and 3 (Washington D.C.: U.S. Government Printing Office, 1971). Other chapters in that excellent manual deal with the analysis of census data, largely from the point of the demographer. Some of the methods discussed in N. H. Carrier and J. Hobcraft, *Demographic Estimation for Developing Societies* (London, 1971) are equally relevant in detecting and correcting errors in nineteenth-century census statistics. The interests of the economic and social historian in respect of British census data are covered in E. A. Wrigley, ed., *Nineteenth-century Society* (Cambridge, 1972). Some of the contributions in that volume discuss in a very clear way the uses that can be made of the manuscript returns (enumerators' books) of the 1851 and 1861 censuses. *The Historical Methods News Letter* (University of Pittsburgh), though concerned mainly with United States material, often contains articles of relevance to historians dealing with British data. A detailed discussion of modern British censuses — methods, concepts and definitions — will be found in B. Benjamin, *The Population Census* (London, 1970).

The most important account of British censuses from 1801 onwards is that by [L. M. Feery], *Census Reports of Great Britain 1801-1931,* 'Guides to Official Sources No. 2' (London: HMSO, 1951). For a discussion of the contemporary reactions to census results and of the arguments about the questions to be included in the census schedules, see M. Drake, 'The census 1801-1891', in E. A. Wrigley, ed., *Nineteenth-century Society.* There are no comparable accounts of the Censuses of Ireland. The two papers by P. Froggatt, cited in the text, refer to the abortive census of 1813-15 and more generally to some aspects of the censuses of 1841 to 1871, in respect of the contributions of Sir William Wilde. Useful information on the history of censuses (and vital registration) will be found in the handbooks prepared for the League of Nations Health Organisation before the war by Major Greenwood and P. Granville Edge, as part of a series, each volume entitled *Official Vital Statistics of....* The relevant volumes are those for England and Wales (Geneva, 1925); for Scotland (Geneva, 1929); and for Ireland (Geneva, 1929).

Contemporary discussion of the various census reports will be found in the main journals of the period. References are given in the text to articles in the *Journal of the Royal Statistical Society*. In addition, Gregg International published a series of volumes, conveniently grouped by main topics, containing reprints of relevant articles from the *Quarterly Review*, the *Edinburgh Review* and from several other major nineteenth-century periodicals. The general Reports on each census, printed as part of the census publications, are especially worth consulting.

Nineteenth-century demographic history

Though there are many articles, both contemporary and modern, on various aspects of the demographic history of Great Britain and Ireland, there are very few general surveys. On Britain the *Report* of the Royal Commission on Population (Cmnd. 7695, London, 1949) should be consulted, though its main concern is with more recent developments. A compilation of basic demographic statistics for Great Britain is given in *Reports and Selected Papers on the Statistics Committee* published in 'Papers of the Royal Commission on Population' (London: HMSO, 1950) Vol. 2, pp. 188-212. Useful statistics will also be found in B. R. Mitchell and P. Deane, *Abstract of British Historical Statistics* (Cambridge, 1962).

A general review of trends in England and Wales, with particular reference to fertility, will be found in Ch. I of D. V. Glass, *Population Policies and Movements in Europe* (Oxford, 1940; reprint London, 1967), which also provides references to many other relevant publications. On population trends in the early nineteenth century, G. T. Griffith, *Population Problems of the Age of Malthus* (Cambridge, 1926; reprint London, 1967); and M. C. Buer, *Health Wealth and Population in the Early Days of the Industrial Revolution* (London, 1926) are still of interest. But they need to be supplemented by more recent studies, the implications of which are discussed most admirably, with ample references, in M. W. Flinn, *British Population Growth 1700-1850* (London, 1970). On Ireland, the earlier period is dealt with in K. H. Connell, *The Population of Ireland 1700-1845* (Oxford, 1950), and the Famine years in R. D. Edwards and T. D. Williams, eds., *The Great Famine. Studies in Irish History 1845-52* (Dublin, 1956). For subsequent developments, see K. H. Connell, *Irish Peasant Society* (Oxford, 1968); and the various Reports of the *Commission on Emigration and other Population Problems* (Dublin: The Stationery Office, 1948-54). A most valuable contribution is that of R. E. Kennedy Jr., *The Irish. Emigration, Marriage and Fertility* (Berkeley, California, 1973). See also B. Walsh, 'An empirical study of the age structure of the Irish population', *The Economic and Social Review*, Vol. 1, No. 2, January 1970; M. Drake, 'Marriage and population growth in Ireland 1750-1845', *Economic History Review*, 2nd series, Vol. 16, No. 2, December 1963; and J. Lee, 'Marriage and population in pre-famine Ireland', *Economic History Review*, 2nd series, Vol. 21, No. 2, August 1968. On fertility, the most comprehensive data, extending back to the mid-nineteenth century, were collected at the 1911 Censuses of Great Britain and Ireland, and are to be found in the census reports. The data for England and Wales are re-examined in J. W. Innes, *Class Fertility Trends in England and Wales, 1876-1934* (Princeton, N.J., 1938). On the control of fertility, see P. Fryer, *The Birth Controllers* (London, 1965). The course of mortality is best studied in the annual

reports of the Registrars-General and in the special decennial supplements
of the Registrar-General of England and Wales. See also W. P. D. Logan,
'Mortality in England and Wales from 1848 to 1947', *Population Studies,*
Vol. 4, Part 2, September 1950; and T. McKeown and R. G. Record,
'Reasons for the decline of mortality in England and Wales during the
nineteenth century', *Population Studies,* Vol. 16, Part 2, November 1962.

Households and Housing

The nineteenth-century census results, as published, contain relatively
little on these topics, and even less on the latter than on the former. (The
Irish censuses provide more information – e.g. on the number of rooms
per household). But the manuscript material of the 1851 and 1861
Censuses have provided the basis for useful local studies. On households
generally, Peter Laslett's introduction to P. Laslett, ed., *Household and
Family in Time Past* (Cambridge, 1972), is an informative discussion of
what was until recently a rather neglected subject. Data for England and
Wales over a long period are used in W. V. Hole and M. T. Pountney,
Trends in Population, Housing and Occupancy Rates 1861-1961 (London:
HMSO, 1971). For the problems involved in assessing changes in
household size and composition over time, see A. Block, *Estimating
Housing Needs* (London, 1946) and R. Glass and F. G. Davidson,
'Household structure and housing needs', *Population Studies,* Vol. 4,
Part 4, March 1951. The housing conditions of the poor are documented
in a very large number of contemporary studies, both official and private.
The best-known single study is, of course, the Chadwick report: *Report
. . . on an Inquiry into the Sanitary Condition of the Labouring Population
of Great Britain* (London, 1842: IUP series Health General, vols. 3 and 4).
(There are in addition separate volumes on England and Wales and on
Scotland.) An excellent modern study of the conditions in London
(including an examination of employment) is that by G. Stedman Jones,
Outcast London (Oxford, 1961). For a general survey of working-class
housing over a long period, see W. V. Hole, *The Housing of the Working
Classes in Britain 1850-1914,* Ph.D., University of London, 1965. M.
Anderson provides a thorough analysis of household structure in Preston
(Lancashire) in the mid-nineteenth century, the enumerators' books being
the primary source material, in *Family Structure in Nineteenth Century
Lancashire* (Cambridge, 1971). References to other local studies are given
in his ample bibliography. On Ireland there is some useful background
material – though the book is primarily concerned with conditions in the
1930s – in C. M. Arensberg and S. T. Kimball, *Family and Community in
Ireland* (2nd edn., Cambridge, Mass., 1968).

Urban growth and urbanization

The most useful general studies are: R. Glass, *Urban Sociology in Britain, a
Trend Report, Current Sociology,* Vol. 4, No. 4, 1955 (containing an
extensive, annotated bibliography of nineteenth- and twentieth-century
publications); W. Ashworth, *The Genesis of Modern British Town Planning*
(London, 1954); and H. J. Dyos, ed., *The Study of Urban History*
(London, 1968). There are, of course, many studies of individual towns,

both before and after Charles Booth's survey of London. For one local study, based especially upon the enumerators' books, see A. Armstrong, *Stability and Change in an English County Town. A Social Study of York 1801-1851,* London 1974. Weber's well-known, comparative survey of of urban growth is still worth reading – A. F. Weber, *The Growth of Cities in the Nineteenth Century* (New York, 1899; reprint Ithaca, N.Y., 1963). See also J.K. Kellett, *The Impact of Railways on Victorian Cities* (London, 1969); and T. Ferguson *et al., Public Health and Urban Growth* (London: Centre for Urban Studies, 1964).

Occupations and employment
These topics are discussed in all major textbooks of economic and social history – e.g. in the various volumes of J. Clapham's *An Economic History of Modern Britain,* 3 vols. (reprinted Cambridge, 1967-68). See also S. G. Checkland, *The Rise of Industrial Society in England, 1815-1885* (London, 1964); H. Perkin, *The Origins of Modern English Society 1780-1880* (London, 1969); and M. J. Reader, *Professional Men: the Rise of the Professional Classes in Nineteenth Century England* (London, 1966). A. L. Bowley, *Wages and Income in the United Kingdom since 1860* (Cambridge, 1937), is a very useful survey and attempts to estimate the growth of the middle class during the period. On Scotland, see: H. A. Marwick, *Economic Developments in Victorian Scotland* (London, 1936); T. Ferguson, *The Dawn of Scottish Social Welfare* (Edinburgh, 1948) and *Scottish Social Welfare, 1864-1914* (Edinburgh, 1958). On Ireland, see: G. A. T. O'Brien, *Economic History of Ireland from the Union to the Famine* (Dublin, 1921) and F. S. L. Lyons, *Ireland since the Famine* (London, 1971). The most detailed attempt to use nineteenth-century census data on occupations is that by W. A. Armstrong in his contribution to E. A. Wrigley, ed., *Nineteenth-century Society* (Cambridge, 1972). See also F. Bedarida, 'Londres au milieu du XIXe siècle: une analyse de structure sociale', *Annales,* Vol. 23, No. 2, 1968. On the employment of women, see M. Hewitt, *Wives and Mothers in Victorian Industry* (London, 1959); I. Pinchbeck, *Women Workers and the Industrial Revolution* (London, 1930); W. F. Neff, *Victorian Working Women* (London, 1929); and L. Davidoff, *The Employment of Married Women in England 1850-1950,* M.A. dissertation, University of London, 1956.

Religion
For a general introduction, see D. Martin, *A Sociology of English Religion* (London, 1967). A specialist study, which also provides information on Ireland as a whole, is that by H. W. Robinson, 'A study of the Church of Ireland population of Ardfert, Co. Kerry, 1971', *The Economic and Social Review,* Vol. 4, No. 1, October 1972. On Scotland, see J. Highet, *The Scottish Churches* (London, 1960) and S. Mechie, *The Church and Scottish Social Development, 1780-1870* (Oxford, 1960). On Ireland, see J. McCaffrey, *History of the Catholic Church in the Nineteenth Century* (Dublin, 1902).

For modern discussions and analyses of the data collected by the 1851 Census of religious attendance, see J. D. Gay, *The Geography of Religion in England* (London, 1971); K. S. Inglis, 'Patterns of religious worship in

1851', *Journal of Ecclesiastical History*, Vol. 11, 1960; W. S. F. Pickering, 'The 1851 religious census: a useless experiment?', *British Journal of Sociology*, Vol. 18, 1967; and D. M. Thompson, 'The 1851 religious census: problems and possibilities', *Victorian Studies*, Vol. 11, 1967. For nineteenth-century analyses of census and survey data on religion, see the various publications of the Reverend Abraham Hume, especially his *Results of the Irish Census of 1861, with a Special Reference to the Church of Ireland* (London, 1864).

Education

For relevant background information on England and Wales, see J. W. Adamson, *English Education* (Cambridge, 1930); F. Smith, *History of English Elementary Education 1760-1902* (London, 1931); H. C. Dent, *1870-1970. Century of Growth in English Education* (London, 1970); and G. A. N. Lowndes, *The Silent Social Revolution*, 2nd edn. (London, 1969). For Scotland, see J. Scotland, *The History of Scottish Education*, 2 vols. (London, 1969) and H. M. Knox, *Two Hundred and Fifty Years of Scottish Education, 1696-1946* (Edinburgh, 1953). There are also specialist studies of the history of education in the individual counties of Scotland – e.g. W. Boyd, *Education in Ayrshire Through Seven Centuries* (London, 1961); and A. Bain, *Education in Stirlingshire from the Reformation to the Act of 1872* (London, 1965). (These studies are sponsored by the Scottish Council for Research in Education.) On Ireland, see J. J. Auchmuty, *Irish Education: an Historical Survey* (Dublin, 1937).

On literacy, see R. K. Webb, *The British Working Class Reader* (London, 1955) and R. K. Webb, 'The Victorian reading public', in B. Ford, ed., *From Dickens to Hardy* (The Pelican guide to English Literature, Vol. 6, Harmondsworth, 1960). C. M. Cipolla, *Literacy and Development in the West* (Harmondsworth, 1969), conveniently brings together a considerable amount of comparative material, though without much analysis. A general survey of the data for England is given in L. Stone, 'Literacy and education in England 1640-1900', *Past and Present*, No. 42, 1969. (It should be remembered that 'literacy' was not reported by the censuses of Great Britain. Such information as is now available is thus derived from other sources, including the analysis of the extent to which marriage registers were signed with the names of the bride and groom or by a mark. The Irish censuses included a question on literacy from 1841 onwards).

Internal migration and immigration

These two topics are covered by a single heading because they are linked by the basic census data, namely the statistics of 'birthplace'. Those statistics show the origin of the foreign-born population (including the population born in Ireland). They also provide the basis for calculating 'lifetime' internal migration and, more recently, have been used by Friedlander and Roshier for estimating intercensal streams of internal migration. The published statistics do not allow such estimates to be constructed below the county level. But the manuscript material from the 1851 and 1861 censuses makes it possible to show distributions of internal migrants and immigrants within communities – for example, by streets within enumeration districts.

On internal migration see E. C. Ravenstein, 'The laws of migration', *J.R.S.S.*, Vols. 48, 1885, and 52, 1889; A. Redford, *Labour Migration in England 1800-1850* (Manchester, 1926); H. A. Shannon, 'Migration and the growth of London 1841-1891', *Economic History Review*, Vol. 5, 1935, A. B. Hill, *Internal Migration and its Effects upon the Death Rates with Special Reference to the County of Essex* (London, 1925); B. Thomas, 'Migration into the Glamorganshire coalfield 1861-1911', *Economica*, Vol. 30, 1930; D. Friedlander and D. J. Roshier, 'A study of internal migration in England and Wales', *Population Studies*, Vol. 19, Part 3, 1966 and Vol. 20, Part 1, 1966; J. Saville, *Rural Depopulation in England and Wales 1851-1951* (London, 1957); D. F. Macdonald, *Scotland's Shifting Population, 1770-1850* (Glasgow, 1937).

On immigration and immigrant communities, a basic source for the late nineteenth century is the Royal Commission on Alien Immigration, *Report and Minutes of Evidence*, 4 vols. (London: HMSO, 1903). (BPP, 1903, IX). For modern studies dealing with various groups, see L. P. Gartner, *The Jewish Immigrant in England 1870-1914* (London, 1960); V. D. Lipman, *Social History of the Jews in England 1850-1950* (London, 1954); B. Gainer, *The Alien Invasion* (London, 1972); J. A. Jackson, *The Irish in Britain* (London, 1963); J. E. Handley, *The Irish in Scotland, 1798-1845* (Cork, 1943) and *The Irish in Modern Scotland* (Cork, 1947); J. Zubrzycki, *Polish Immigrants in Britain* (London, 1956); K. Little, *Negroes in Britain* (London, 1948; revised edn. London, 1972); R. Glass, *Newcomers: the West Indian in London* (London, 1960); R. Glass, (ed.), *London − Aspects of Change* (London, 1964).

A detailed bibliography on British emigration by Dr. P. A. M. Taylor will be found on pp. 117-120 of this publication.

EMIGRATION

P. A. M. Taylor

Contents

EMIGRATION

Commentary

Introduction: Emigration and Government in the Nineteenth Century

In 1815, the British Empire emerged from a long war with France and from a short one with the United States. Its territories included places, like Malta and Gibraltar, of purely strategic significance; areas, especially the Indian provinces, already densely occupied by a long-established native population; the West Indies where a small planter class controlled a mass of black slaves imported during the previous two centuries; Cape Colony where there was both a native population and a distinct non-British white element; Lower Canada which was largely French; Upper Canada and the Maritimes, backwoods colonies peopled quite largely from the United States; and small Australian settlements most of whose inhabitants were transported convicts. Britain itself was at an early stage of its Industrial Revolution, the stage, indeed, at which social conditions were probably at their grimmest. The highly conservative governments of the day might interest themselves in emigration in response to an American threat to Canada, from a desire to outweigh convict population, or with a view to relieving discontent at home sufficiently to reduce radical protest.

Individual Britons, to be sure, had their own varied reasons for wishing to leave their native land, whether a desire for cheap farms, for the accustomed industrial job at higher wages, or for escape from some special crisis at home.[1] Such emigrants faced conditions very different from those encountered by people who, in the very same years, were flooding into the American West. They could not plod along trails with their waggons, nor float down rivers in home-made flatboats. Instead, they had to embark in wooden sailing ships and cross oceans, with all the discomforts and dangers then entailed. Given these difficulties, and conditions in the colonies, it was all too likely that the people best fitted to succeed would be precisely those who could make good at home, while those in Britain who clamoured for aid to leave would be the least fitted to prosper, or even survive, overseas.

At a time when the crossing from Liverpool to New York averaged five weeks, and one to Quebec or New Orleans only a few days more, it commonly took ten weeks to reach the Cape and four months to arrive at Sydney. Yet the United States was much more developed than any part of the overseas Empire, and its abundant economic opportunities were

---

1 The most interesting, and the most authoritative, source is now the introductions to the collections of emigrant letters in Charlotte Erickson, *Invisible Immigrants: the adaptation of English and Scottish immigrants in 19th century America* (London, 1972).

supplemented by republican institutions which appealed to many, while it could be expected that New South Wales in the convict era might be the least popular field for free emigrants. The result was that the favourite destination was the cheapest to reach, and the least appealing was the dearest: hence the emigration of honest citizens to Australia was always likely to require government aid.

Although many of these problems had to be worked out by each individual and family unaided — and little of this has left any documentary trace — government was involved at many points; and a few words are needed about the forms of government then in existence. Except in the West Indies, where old-style Assemblies survived, Governors from noble families or from the higher ranks of the armed forces ruled with the help of Executive Councils alone, or faced Legislative Councils composed of official nominees with a very slowly rising proportion of elected men. In most colonies, 'Family Compacts' of officials and privileged persons were likely to exist, which Governors might or might not be able to control in pursuit of policies laid down in their instructions from home.[2] Self-government developed as the century advanced; and by the 1850s most of the colonies important to British emigrants had governments responsible to fairly widely based legislatures. In London, the Colonial Office had a very small staff, no more than three dozen of all ranks in 1831.[3] In making appointments overseas, it faced a shortage of trained men. In communicating with those appointed, it was hampered by the slow speed of transport, for between an event in New South Wales calling for a decision, and the arrival of that decision in the colony, a whole year might pass. Equally damaging, the Colonial Office was far from the most important department of the government, nor were Colonial Secretaries the leading figures in cabinets. Very often, therefore, well-considered plans were vetoed by the far more powerful Treasury;[4] for nowadays the expenditure of millions is authorized far more readily than, in those days, the spending of a few hundred pounds.

Since this Commentary deals with a whole century and with a large part of the world, it must select quite ruthlessly from infinitely complex events and documents; and it will help the reader, at this point, to outline the

2   For Upper Canada, where the system was particularly notorious, see Peter Burroughs, *The Canadian Crisis and British Colonial Policy, 1828-1841* (London, 1972).

3   D. Murray Young, *The Colonial Office in the Early Nineteenth Century* (London, 1961), pp. 278-79.

4   Oliver MacDonagh, *A Pattern of Government Growth: the Passenger Acts and their Enforcement, 1800-60* (London, 1961), pp. 257-65, provides an excellent example. There is also much information in D. M. Young, *The Colonial Office*, chs. 6 and 7.

principal trends in nineteenth-century emigration, before embarking upon a detailed discussion of the documents and their relation to history.[5]

The long war with France broke the continuity of an emigration movement which had been important in the later eighteenth century. The 1820s saw very small numbers, the 1830s much larger ones; but the first great bulge occurred with the Irish famine of the next decade: two and a half million people emigrated in eight years. A decline set in during the later 1850s; there was some revival in the 1860s; and a new peak was reached in the years immediately either side of 1870. The biggest numbers of all went during the 1880s, and the decline that followed lasted until the century's end. As to the emigrants' origins, Ulster was very prominent in the early decades, just as it had been in the eighteenth century.[6] Catholic Ireland dominated the century's middle years. From about 1870, England and Scotland were consistently in the lead. As for destinations, British North America was especially prominent in the 1830s, and led the United States, by a narrow margin, for the period 1815-40 as a whole. With the Famine, however, the United States went far ahead, and thereafter the proportion between it and Canada was likely to be five, or even as high as nine, to one. The Australian colonies took many emigrants in the very early 1840s, in the 1850s after the gold rush, and again in the early 1860s. In a very few single years, Australian figures for British emigrants alone came close to the American and were far ahead of the Canadian; but usually they were no higher than a third of the American total. After the 1880s, Australia was in depression; Canadian figures became the higher; and they remained so well into the twentieth century, since Australia experienced its next immigration boom only just before World War I. Emigration, too, underwent changes in technology and organization. It saw growing specialization of passenger vessels – on the North Atlantic, principally American vessels – in the 1850s; growing concentration at Liverpool and New York; then, in the 1860s, the triumph of steam on the North Atlantic, and on other oceans in the next quarter-century.[7] As for

5   For the framework of fact, it is sufficient to refer to three authorities: *Perspectives in American History*, VII (1973), which contains long essays by Maldwyn Jones on British emigration to the United States, by Malcolm Gray on the Scottish Lowlands, and by Alan Conway on Welsh emigration; N. M. Carrier and J. R. Jeffery, *External Migration: a Study in the Available Statistics* (London, 1953) and Brinley Thomas, *Migration and Economic Growth* (Cambridge, 1954).

6   R. J. Dickson, *Ulster Emigration to Colonial America, 1718-1775* (London, 1966); Maldwyn A. Jones, 'Ulster Emigration, 1783-1815', in *Essays in Scotch-Irish History*, ed. E. R. R. Green (London, 1969), pp. 48-68; William F. Adams, *Ireland and Irish Emigration to the New World from 1815 to the Famine* (New Haven, 1932).

7   A sufficient summary of these changes may be found in Philip Taylor, *The Distant Magnet: European Emigration to the United States* (London, 1971), chs. 7 and 8.

official policy, the first years after 1815 saw direct financial aid to emigration by the British government, though on a very small scale, with Canada chiefly in view. Then came a period in which, under a considerable degree of British control, colonial land revenues were used to pay for emigrants' passages, and this affected chiefly the Australian colonies. From the 1850s, however, with advancing self-government, each colony assumed control of its own land policy and therefore of emigration finance. Side by side with all this, of course, went a very much larger emigration financed by individuals — much of the Australian movement and almost all the North American. In that area of emigration, government was involved in a different way, building up and trying to enforce a system of protective law.

Changes in policy and organization in turn exerted an influence upon the records of the overseas movement. The earliest experiments were soon followed by large-scale investigations in the 1820s and 1830s. From 1840, the Colonial Land and Emigration Commission was the central institution. With colonial self-government, the Commission began to lose its functions; and in the 1870s, after the Board of Trade had taken over the task of enforcing the Passenger Acts, it went out of existence. Instead, therefore, of annual reports and innumerable other documents, which characterize the three middle decades of the nineteenth century, there now appear no more than annual statistics together with a handful of official inquiries. Counting both the Emigration series and those Colonies volumes in which emigration is a prominent subject, the ratio of documentation between the three periods 1800-39, 1840-73, and 1874-1900 is roughly two : five : one.

A few words must be said about the student's problems in handling this material. The Irish University Press editors have consolidated documents into an Emigration series; but in a facsimile edition they have naturally felt bound to follow the original subdivision into Reports of Commissions, Reports of Committees, and Accounts and Papers. The Colonial Land and Emigration Commissioners' reports appear as a single series, but information on any one year will be widely separated from other documents dealing with the same year or the same transaction, which happen to be part of an investigation or a despatch. Developments, therefore, often have to be traced from volume to volume, numbered sometimes at opposite ends of the series. A further editorial decision must be noted. Each year in the original parliamentary papers documents were printed relating to the several colonies; and anyone studying these areas for their own sake will be grateful that the arrangement has been retained in the Colonies sets. The student of emigration, however, has to seek information, about policy-making, about background conditions, and about the arrival of emigrants, in the parliamentary papers on Canada or Australia. Once at least, a single series of important documents, A. C. Buchanan's reports from Quebec, has to be traced from one series to another and back again: 1831-39 in Emigration 19 and 20; 1840-43 in Canada 15 and 16; 1844 (a summary only) in Emigration 10 (the Commissioners' fifth report). and 1846-61 in Canada 17 to 24; while the reports for 1833 and 1845 are nowhere to be seen.

Two further technicalities should be observed. A despatch, whether from a Governor or a Secretary of State, commonly has enclosures, consisting of reports on which the decision has been based. These in turn may contain sub-enclosures, containing the raw material out of which they have been compiled. For any such transaction, the real order of events is likely to be the reverse of the order in which documents appear in our volumes. Second, although in early years despatches were immediately followed by replies regardless of date, from mid-century the characteristic plan was to print all colonial despatches in a single year's block, then all the Secretary of State's replies, then on to the next colony.[8] In a year of complex business, therefore, not only do the two sides of a transaction appear many pages apart, but, because of the time-lag noted above, may have to be searched for in an earlier or a later volume.

When he has mastered these problems, and arranged the material to meet his own needs, the researcher will naturally go on to assess the comprehensiveness and reliability of the papers before him. This Commentary will conclude with a long section seeking to help him reach conclusions on these matters; but first it will be necessary to relate, in a more general way, the documents with the several periods of emigration, before, during and after the years of the Commissioners' work.

The Period of Experiment

Ever since the acquisition of Canada from the French at the close of the Seven Years' War, the British government had been interested in encouraging British settlement, whether to reward loyal individuals with land, to balance the French society which already existed, or to build up a colony that could resist the persuasion or coercion of the United States.[9] After 1815, another motive appeared, a willingness to use emigration so as

8 Contrast the arrangement of *South Australia: Correspondence between Governor Grey and Lord John Russell*, 1843 [505], XXXII; IUP Colonies: Australia 7, pp. 23-362, with *Papers relating to Australia 1852-53*, 1852-53 [1627], LXVIII; IUP Colonies: Australia 17.

9 Norman Macdonald, *Canada 1763-1841, Immigration and Settlement: the Administration of the Imperial Land Regulations* (London, 1939), chs. ii, iii, iv; H. J. M. Johnston, *British Emigration Policy, 1815-1830* (Oxford, 1972), ch. i.

to relieve distress at home. Two methods presented themselves. One was the application of British government funds, so as to pay for the Atlantic crossing and provide accommodation, implements and rations on the lands assigned. The other was to grant large acreages to individual or corporate promoters, who would recruit and organize, taking their profit from the lease or re-sale of land to settlers. Either kind of colonization enterprise bristled with difficulties. A land company was all too likely to plead insuperable problems as an excuse for evading its obligations. A single promoter might prove incompetent or, like Thomas Talbot, might arouse antagonism by the authoritarianism that accompanied his undoubted ability. Direct aid, on the other hand, required the appointment of skilled men to plan the settlement and care for inexperienced colonists in the early days; and it was costly, in days when governments were notably economy-minded. The settlers faced an ocean journey, a dense forest, undeveloped communications, and an unfamiliar climate; and if they became discouraged, they were likely to desert in search of the more abundant opportunities across the American border. All these circumstances were complicated by the existence of a narrowly oligarchical government in Canada, and by a system of Crown and Clergy Reserves which hampered and separated those who wished to subdue the wilderness by systematic cultivation.[10]

Very soon after 1815, small numbers of Scots were established in Upper Canada, joining the earlier settlements of disbanded soldiers and American Loyalists. In the early 1820s, further contingents were sent from the distressed population of the Glasgow region. In 1823 and 1825, larger numbers of Irish were organized by Peter Robinson and taken to the same general destination.[11]

By that time, the Parliamentary Under-Secretary at the Colonial Office was Wilmot Horton, an ambitious politician who for years tried to combine the aims of relieving distress in Britain and promoting colonial growth. He was not convinced by the Malthusian argument that the good results of emigration would quickly be offset by a rise in the British birth-rate: relief from the burden of pauperism would be permanent. It was he who gave Robinson his task. It was he who took the leading part in the Committees of 1826 and 1827. He urged a very broad programme of emigration, financed in Britain by borrowing on the security of the

10   N. Macdonald, *Canada 1763-1841*, chs. v (Talbot and Selkirk), vi (the Reserves), vii (land companies). For fuller detail, see Lillian F. Gates, *Land Policies of Upper Canada* (Toronto: 1968) and Alan Wilson, *The Clergy Reserves of Upper Canada: a Canadian Mortmain* (Toronto, 1968).

11   Helen I. Cowan, *British Emigration to British North America: the First Hundred Years*, rev. ed. (Toronto, 1961), esp. chs. iii and iv; H. J. M. Johnston, *British Emigration Policy*, chs. ii and iii.

poor-rate, and in Ireland, as yet with no Poor Law system, by the landlords who would then be able to rationalize their estates. In either case the aim was identical: to spend money to remove paupers (and strengthen colonies) instead of to maintain them indefinitely at home. The government, however, could not bring itself to undertake work on such a scale; and neither parish- nor landlord-aided emigration ever attained really large dimensions.[12]

While these enterprises were under consideration for Canada and the Maritimes, New South Wales and Van Diemen's Land continued to be dominated by convicts. Some of these provided direct labour on roads and other public works: most were assigned to landowners or occupiers of sheep-runs.[13] To introduce free settlers, in numbers that could rival those of the felons, would call for a revised land policy, assistance for emigration, and very probably the ending of transportation itself.

Before such a thing could occur, a private venture was undertaken at the other end of the continent, the Swan River settlement of Western Australia. A promoter was granted a large area of land in return for bringing in a prescribed number of settlers and establishing them upon it.[14] The land companies of a few years earlier, in New South Wales and Van Diemen's Land, also involved, like their counterparts in Canada, a delegation to private interests of responsibility for migration and economic development.[15]

Almost at once, however, a new element appeared, a group of men with a theory, who lobbied in government circles, undertook propaganda, attacked rival views with vast ability and considerable lack of scruple, and in a few years did much to change the direction of British policy. The original thinker among them was Edward Gibbon Wakefield. He saw that underdeveloped areas needed to attract capital, managerial skill, and labour. He asserted that these could be employed most effectively in concentrated units. Yet the tendency in such a society was for capitalists to acquire, by grant, more land than they could use, and for labourers to become subsistence farmers rather than working for employers. The

12 *Report from the Select Committee on Emigration from the United Kingdom*, 1826 (404), IV, and *First, Second and Third Reports from the Select Committee, . . .* 1826-27 (88), (237), (550), V; IUP Emigration 1 and 2. See also H. J. M. Johnston, *British Emigration Policy*, chs. iv (Horton), vi, vii (the Committees), viii and ix (the plans and their fate).

13 A. G. L. Shaw, *Convicts and Colonies* (London, 1966); Stephen H. Roberts, *History of Australian Land Settlement, 1788-1920* (Melbourne, 1924), Part I; Ronald M. Hartwell, *The Economic Development of Van Diemen's Land, 1820-1850* (Melbourne, 1954).

14 James S. Battye, *Western Australia: a History* (Oxford, 1924), esp. pp. 74-95.

15 S. H. Roberts, *Australian Land Settlement*, pp. 52-69.

United States, he thought, escaped the worst consequences of its abundance of land on the frontier, but only by producing its chief export crops with slave labour. Very soon he was singling out Swan River as the example above all others of how not to found a colony. As a remedy, Wakefield put his faith in planning the price of land. The price would doubtless vary from one colony to another; but in each it would be set at a point that would compel men to work for wages for a few years before they could acquire independence. Capitalists would thus have a reserve of labour with which to launch productive farming and other enterprises. A valuable by-product, however, would be the appearance of a land revenue. On the security of such a fund, governments could borrow; and although such money might contribute to general public needs, much or most of it would be used to assist emigration. If people with appropriate skills could be found, and especially young married couples who would have their children in the colonies, then both the surplus of labour at home and the primitive economic condition of the colonies might be remedied.[16] If a single sentence can sum up such a doctrine, it is Charles Buller's in a House of Commons debate in 1843:

When I ask you to colonize, what do I ask you to do but to employ the superfluity of one part of our country to repair the deficiency of the other: to cultivate the desert by applying to it the means that lie idle here: to convey the plough to the field, the workman to his work, the hungry to his food.[17]

Almost at once, the new ideas began to take effect, changing official minds or giving coherence to administrators' tentatively formulated plans. In 1831 the Colonial Office ruled in favour of selling colonial land rather than granting it, though the price was too low for Wakefield's taste. Australian funds were used to finance a small female emigration. For a short time, Emigration Commissioners were appointed, chiefly to distri-

16 I base my summary upon Wakefield's evidence before the *Select Committee on the Disposal of Lands in British Colonies,* 1836 (512), XI; IUP Colonies: General 2, pp. 185-451. For extended modern description and discussion, see R. C. Mills, *The Colonization of Australia, 1829-42: the Wakefield Experiment in Empire-Building* (London, 1915), esp. ch. v; S. H. Roberts, *Australian Land Settlement,* pp. 77-92 (stressing changes in the doctrine through time); Peter Burroughs, *Britain and Australia, 1831-1855: a Study in Imperial Relations and Crown Lands Administration* (Oxford, 1967); Donald Winch, *Classical Political Economy and Colonies* (London, 1965), chs. vi to ix.

17 *Hansard,* Third Series, lxviii, col. 503, quoted in A. Grenfell Price, *The Foundation and Settlement of South Australia* (Adelaide, 1924), p. 1.

bute reliable information about opportunities overseas and the character of the journey.[18]

It was quite independent of the Commission, however, that moves were made towards more effective protection of emigrants as a whole. The provisions of the Passenger Acts of 1828 and 1835 were rudimentary: a set ratio of passengers to the size of vessels, precautions as to seaworthiness, a supply of bread and water, subsistence money for passengers delayed, and a rather vague specification about a medicine chest. The second law was in a sense a response to the cholera epidemic of 1832. More immediately, however, it resulted from the appointment, at local request, of an Emigration Officer at Liverpool, a man who, working at first under ill-defined rules and always in danger of being attacked for exceeding his powers, strove to have the law improved so as to equip himself to remedy the abuses he could see.[19] A very powerful force was thus established, which would soon bring about far more comprehensive regulation.

The Wakefield group now launched the settlement of South Australia, with a twelve shilling per acre minimum price for land. In the short run, the colony was hampered by disputes about the exact location, by inadequate survey staff, by divided responsibility between officers; and after a few years, overspending resulted in the British government's taking over full control. In the long run, however, South Australia became a prosperous settlement, with wheat as the central product — an economy with a balance quite different from that of New South Wales.[20]

In 1837, a more positive attempt was made to introduce co-ordination in emigration matters, South Australia apart. T. F. Elliot was appointed Agent-General; and although collecting and distributing information remained a primary task, he also began conducting an assisted emigration to New South Wales. His first Report shows agents travelling through England's rural counties to recruit workers, the publication of notices about terms and organization, and the taking of decisions about surgeon-superintendents for the ships.[21] At the same time, there arose an Australian emigration conducted on different principles. This was the Bounty system, by which settlers were to name the categories of workers

---

18 *Emigration Commissioners: Reports to the Secretary of State for the Colonial Department,* 1831-32 (724), XXXII; IUP Emigration 19, pp. 133-62. The best secondary source is now P. Burroughs, *Britain and Australia,* ch. ii.

19 O. Macdonagh, *Pattern of Government Growth,* pp. 75-7 (1828 Act), 88-90 (1835 Act), chs. 5 and 6 (Low and his colleagues of the 1830s).

20 The full history is in A. G. Price, *South Australia.*

21 *Report from the Agent-General for Emigration to the Secretary of State for the Colonies,* 1837-38 (388), XL; IUP Emigration 19, pp. 377-401.

they needed, purchase bounty orders for them, have them selected in Britain, and obtain refunds as soon as the newcomers had been found, by inspection on arrival, to meet the requirements laid down. In practice, the system became dominated by shipowners, especially John Marshall; but the colonists long remained convinced that the Bounty system exactly met their needs.[22]

The decade of the 1830s, then, saw a number of advances for which Wakefield and his associates hastened to claim credit. They exaggerated their influence, and many historians have followed them. What occurred did not always follow their predictions. Successes could sometimes be explained in other terms: Western Australia's slow development, and South Australia's greater success, resulted from soil conditions and similar factors and not merely the land system – after all, Western Australia had a system of sale and not of grant after a very few years. The Wakefield theories had nothing to say about the optimum unit of land in any colony, a factor which was of critical importance in early Natal; nor of course did they provide any formula to ensure a market for produce, despite their emphasis on agricultural production. To make one further point, they were not very relevant to a sheep-raising economy, with its special ratio between land, capital and labour.[23] Having stated all these limitations, however, it must be admitted that one more triumph for the Wakefield group lay ahead, and probably the greatest of all.

This resulted from the Canadian rebellions of 1837. Lord Durham, sent out to investigate, took Charles Buller officially and Wakefield himself unofficially, to help him report on land questions. The full report, and Buller's companion piece which was overwhelmingly Wakefield's, launched a powerful attack on the conduct of emigration, on the existing land system, and on methods of government. A prominent feature was a most unfavourable comparison between Canada's growth and that of the United States. Only quotation can convey the power of Durham's style, though the reader will also detect much that is misleading:

On the American side, all is activity and bustle. The forest has been

22 Descriptions of the system may be found in Lord Stanley's despatch to Governor Gipps, 14 October 1841, in *Correspondence between the Colonial Office and the Authorities in the Colonies relating to Emigration*, pp. 1-5, 1842 (301), XXXI; IUP Emigration 21, pp. 41-5; *Report from the Select Committee of the House of Lords on Colonization from Ireland*, 1847 (737), (737-II), VI: IUP Emigration 4, Qq. 4421-22 (Elliot), 4529-62 (Carter); Robert B. Madgwick, *Immigration into Eastern Australia 1788-1851* (London, 1937), ch. viii.

23 Nor did Wakefield's prescriptions always command colonial assent: New South Wales denounced the high price of land as a cause of the depression of the 1840s. P. Burroughs, *Britain and Australia*, pp. 120-32, shows, however, that the period of land grants in the colony saw such discrimination against small men as to damage them quite as much as any 'sufficient price' could do.

widely cleared; every year numerous settlements are formed, and thousands of farms are created out of the waste; the country is intersected by common roads; canals and railroads are finished, or in the course of formation . . . Every village has its schoolhouse and place of public worship. Every town has many of both, with its township buildings, its book stores, and probably one or two banks and newspapers . . . On the British side of the line . . . all seems waste and desolate. There is but one railroad in all British America, and that . . . is only 15 miles long. The ancient city of Montreal, which is naturally the commercial capital of the Canadas, will not bear the least comparison, in any respect, with Buffalo, which is the creation of yesterday . . .

Canada's stagnation, Durham asserted in pure Wakefield language, was caused by an erroneous land system, which scattered settlement and discouraged organized enterprise.[24]

Results came quickly. Canadian government was remodelled. Land laws for the colonies were revised.[25] The several strands in the organization and protection of emigrants were brought together. The South Australian Commissioners disappeared. All emigration and land business was to be centralized, as far as London was concerned, in a new institution, the Colonial Land and Emigration Commission, reporting to the Colonial Office.

The Colonial Land and Emigration Commissioners

The documents marking the foundation, in 1840, of the Colonial Land and Emigration Commission emphasize the duty to provide accurate information about prospects in the colonies, and especially about colonial lands; but far more than land came to be involved.[26] The Commissioners organized a large-scale emigration to the Australian and other colonies; they advised the Secretary of State for the Colonies, assembled informa-

24 *Report on the Affairs of British North America from the Earl of Durham*, p. 75, 1839 (3), (139), (303), XVII; IUP Colonies: Canada 2, p. 75. Buller's report ranks as Appendix B.

25 On land questions, see P. Burroughs, *Britain and Australia*, ch. vii. For the general influence of the Report, see the contrasting interpretations in Charles P. Lucas, ed., *Lord Durham's Report on the Affairs of British North America*, 3 vols. (Oxford, 1912), Vol. I and esp. chs. vi, vii (though there is little on *immediate* influence); and Ged Martin, *The Durham Report and British Policy: a Critical Essay* (Cambridge, 1972). Neither is much concerned with emigration policy.

26 *Copies of Commissions appointing several Land and Emigration Commissioners*, 1840 (35), XXXIII; IUP Emigration 20, pp. 215-24. [N.B. The table of contents in this volume has incorrect pagination.] Fred H. Hitchins, *The Colonial Land and Emigration Commission* (Philadelphia, 1931), ch. iii, deals with the early Commissioners and the staff below them.

tion for Parliament and gave evidence before select committees; they enlightened the emigrants themselves; and for people emigrating to all destinations they tried to regulate conditions at the ports and promote safety and welfare on the high seas. In three decades they sent out, in round figures, a third of a million British emigrants in more than eleven hundred ships. They carried a rather larger number of Indian labourers to Mauritius, and another quarter of a million Indians, Chinese and others to the West Indies. Under their general protective system, six and a half million emigrants (including many thousands of foreigners) embarked at British ports, most of them to the United States but a million and a half to British North America and two-thirds of a million to Australia.[27] Most of the movement, of course, can be attributed to the decisions and efforts of individuals and families; but the Commissioners exercised a range of responsibilities quite incompatible with any stereotype of *laissez-faire.* [28]

The Commissioners' 208-page report of 1855 gives a good impression of the scope of their work in the middle decades of the nineteenth century.[29] Its opening pages summarize the previous year's emigration: nearly a third of a million people including some 28,000 Germans and Scandinavians had passed through British ports. From Liverpool alone 50,000 had gone to the United States (241 sailings), as well as 40,000 to the Australian colonies and 15,000 to British North America; yet because of American depression there were already signs of a decline, and by the end of 1854 13,000 people had come back. The Report goes on to treat the financing of emigration. Nearly one and three-quarter millions had flowed back in remittances from North America, and it was accepted that the true sum was much higher. More than £800,000 had been sent by colonial

27 *Thirty-third General Report of the Colonial Land and Emigration Commissioners,* Appendices 10 to 21, 1873 [c.768], XVIII; IUP Emigration 18, pp. 62-84 (there is no continuous pagination in the volumes devoted to these Reports). Since 1815, the total movement from British ports had been seven and a half million: one million before the Commissioners began their work, two million by 1848, three by 1852, four by 1854, five by 1862, six by 1866, and seven by 1870.

28 The argument has been fully developed in O. MacDonagh, *Pattern of Government Growth,* esp. chs. 15 and 16.

29 *Fifteenth General Report of the Colonial Land and Emigration Commissioners,* 1854-55 [1953], XVII; IUP Emigration 12. Occupations of people going to each principal destination appear for the first time in 1856, though the two previous years are covered. Other Reports are full of land questions, financing of emigration, plans for revising protective laws, recruiting labourers for the West Indies. The 1843 Report has much on the depression in New South Wales, that of 1846 on the problems of Australian squatters, that of 1852 on the Victoria gold rush. The 1859 and 1860 Reports deal at length with the gold rush along the Fraser River in British Columbia. The 1865 Report notes that a majority of emigrants are now crossing the Atlantic in steamships (by 1870 the proportion exceeded 95 per cent) and that of 1870 shows English emigrants exceeding Irish for the first time since long before the Famine.

governments, from the proceeds of land sales, to provide for assisted or free passages. To Australia, about half of the 80,000 emigrants had sailed in the 127 vessels chartered by the Commissioners. The Report touches upon mortality at sea, then discusses land and emigration policy colony by colony. Sixty-three appendices follow. The early ones are statistical, classifying emigrants by country and port of departure, and by national origin, as well as by destination. For the government emigration, there is additional information about age, conjugal condition, and occupations, and some detail is given for each ship. Tabulation of coolie emigration is almost equally elaborate. Then statistics of a simpler kind are given for the years since 1815. Information is printed about colonial assistance schemes; tables are printed of shipwrecks and deaths at sea; the new American Passenger Act is summarized, and the proposed British law is briefly discussed. Later appendices treat economic growth in each colony, as well as emigration matters proper. The West Indian sections include complex codes of regulations for coolies working on the plantations of St. Lucia, British Guiana and Trinidad.

More thorough descriptions must be given of selected activities, if the Commissioners' executive, investigatory and advisory roles are to be understood; and it is logical to begin with their planned Australian emigration.

News flowed in regularly from the colonies about the need for labour and the resources that existed for financing emigration. The Governor's despatches might enclose lengthy reports from committees of Legislative Councils and even minutes of evidence presented to them. So the opinions of leading settlers and officials could be seen.[30] Colonial reports of more regular and routine description provided details of wages and prices, and in 1848 such conditions for workers were based on returns sent in by local magistrates.[31] Most of the government-organized emigration was financed from land revenue. Funds from land sales, or borrowings based upon them, were sent to Britain, where the Commissioners selected emigrants and gave them varying degrees of aid. People paying their own passages might be compensated with orders for land. Those depositing money for land within a colony might be allowed to nominate friends and relations,

---

30   An example is in *Correspondence between the Colonial Office and Authorities in the Colonies relating to Emigration*, pp. 37-46, 60-111, 1842 (301), XXXI; IUP Emigration 21, pp. 77-86, 100-151. See also the several references in note 92 below.

31   *Papers Relating to Emigration to the Australian Colonies*, pp. 76-9, 1850 [1163], XL; IUP Colonies: Australia 11, pp. 492-5. This is the Appendix to Merewether's report as Immigration Agent at Sydney.

public funds making up a proportion of the cost if the nominees met certain standards.[32]

Given such extensive use of colonial funds, it was essential to send out only those who could be of use to the colonial economy. The Commissioners' Report of 1842 defined the selection principles as follows:

> that their trades and occupations should be suited to the wants of the colonists; that their ages should be such that their labour may be available to the colonies for some years to come; that their families be not too numerous, both on account of the objections to them by colonial employers, and also because mortality is so likely to arise amongst young children on the voyage; that unmarried females should go under proper protection; and lastly that the sexes should be in equal proportions. It is possible that our selections would be more popular to the colonists if we could include among them a greater number of single men. But the extent of the disproportion of the sexes in the Australian colonies is already so great that it probably ought on no account to be increased.[33]

Unofficial emigration normally contained a preponderance of men; and the Commissioners tried to correct this in the interests of a stable and healthy colonial society. Their 1856 Report includes these emphatic words:

> For the permanent growth of a colonial population every single man who is sent out in excess of the number of single women is absolutely useless. He is a mere sojourner, furnishing a temporary convenience to his employer, and, while he lives, increasing to the extent of his individual labour the annual produce of the colony, but leaving nothing

32   Alternatively, official channels could be used to transmit remittances to individuals at home. Valuable examples of financial methods are to be found in the following documents: *Papers relating to Emigration to the Australian Colonies*, pp. 1-5, 13, 21, 1852 [1489], XXXIV; IUP Colonies: Australia 14 (this volume has no continuous pagination); *Fourteenth General Report of the Colonial Land and Emigration Commissioners*, pp. 129-41, 1854 [1833], XXVIII; IUP Emigration 12; *Seventeenth General Report of the Colonial Land and Emigration Commissioners*, p. 25, 1857 Sess. 2 [2249], XVI; IUP Emigration 13 (the failure of a New South Wales scheme for repayment out of wages of a proportion of the aid extended); *Eighteenth General Report of the Colonial Land and Emigration Commissioners*, pp. 1857-58 [2395], XXIV; IUP Emigration 13.

33   *General Report of the Colonial Land and Emigration Commissioners*, p. 18, 1842 (567), XXV; IUP Emigration 10. Appendices to the Commissioners' Reports show clearly how much higher was the mortality among young children than other passengers. For a particularly grim example, on board vessels carrying soldiers' families to India after the Mutiny, see *Twentieth General Report of the Colonial Land and Emigration Commissioners*, p. 17-20, 1860 [2696], XXIX; IUP Emigration 14.

to replace him when he dies. And to the morality of the colony we need hardly observe an overwhelming excess of men is fraught with the greatest danger.[34]

The result of all these considerations was to require only a very small contribution from farm labourers, shepherds, 'country mechanics' (carpenters, blacksmiths, wheelwrights and the like) with wives and no more than two small children; and larger contributions from less favoured workers, from older people, and from those with additional children, to the point where men and women over fifty would be paying almost a full fare. Single female domestic servants were of course accepted as forming part of the most desired category.[35]

This looks a logical policy; but decisions could not always show consistency over long periods of time. In 1852, for example, the authorities in Victoria wanted all government emigration suspended until it could be seen whether the gold rush would bring about a large enough unassisted movement; but within six months they changed their minds.[36] Nor was harmony always achieved between interests. The Bounty system of the late 1830s and early 1840s was intended to involve settlers' deposits, specification of the types of worker they needed, selection in Britain, and repayment from public funds when the emigrants arrived in the colony and were found to meet the criteria laid down. In pactice, bounty orders were at once taken over by large shipowners, though later on some less reputable firms sought to compete.[37] Colonists tended to think the system excellent in providing a labour force: the British government was likely to see the possibilities of abuse in a system so far removed from its control. In October 1838, for example, the Immigration Committee of the New South Wales Legislative Council extolled the system's merits as against the parallel system of direct government organization. The Immigration Agent at Sydney, Pinnock, insisted that it

34 *Sixteenth General Report of the Colonial Land and Emigration Commissioners*, p. 18, 1856 [2089], XXIV; IUP Emigration 13.

35 From among many examples, the following may be selected: *Ninth General Report of the Colonial Land and Emigration Commissioners*, Appendix 4, 1849 [1082], XXII; IUP Emigration 11; *Twenty-fifth General Report of the Colonial Land and Emigration Commissioners*, Appendix 50, 1865 [3526], XVIII; IUP Emigration 16. The system of assisted passages to the Cape of Good Hope favoured a somewhat wider range of occupations, *Eighteenth General Report of the Colonial Land and Emigration Commissioners*, pp. 222-26, 1857-58 [2395], XXIV; IUP Emigration 13.

36 *Twelfth General Report of the Colonial Land and Emigration Commissioners*, pp. 24-6, 1852 [1499], XVIII; IUP Emigration 11.

37 In addition to the references cited in note 22 above, see the form of tender for Bounty emigration (which by 1843 had come under closer control) in *General Report of the Colonial Land and Emigration Commissioners*, p. 39, 1843 (621), XXIX; IUP Emigration 10.

was more economical, had better ratios of women and children, and was more certain to bring in people with useful skills. Agent-General T. F. Elliot in Britain disagreed; and Dr. Inches, a selecting officer, undermined Pinnock's argument by insisting that people of optimum age and skill, and without children, were precisely those least likely to feel the need to emigrate, whatever Edward Gibbon Wakefield might have said. Throughout 1839 and 1840 the Governor was forwarding colonial views of the usual kind, while Lord John Russell was replying to Gipps with despatches based on the Agent-General's advice. Soon the situation was changed by the onset of depression in New South Wales. Backed by his Council, Gipps continued to urge expansion. In July 1841 Russell is found rebuking the Governor for issuing bounty orders far beyond the capacity of the declining land revenue to meet. Gipps tried hard to meet the arguments; but before his message could reach London the new Colonial Secretary, Stanley, sent an even more peremptory despatch, insisting that bounty orders must cease.[38]

As far as they were directly responsible for selection, the Commissioners faced difficult problems. In 1852, they were using the services of their own former officer, Lieutenant Hodder, at Cork, of more than thirty civilians in Ireland and the south and east of England, and of two dozen Army staff officers, responsible for pensions and possessing much local knowledge, to cover the rest of the British Isles.[39] This large establishment was made necessary by the expansion of emigration based upon buoyant Australian land revenue; but recruiting faced the obstacle of good employment prospects in Britain. Indeed, as the Commissioners explained, there always existed a conflict between colonial demand and British supply:

Paupers, as they are generally called, are below the required class,

---

38   The controversy may be followed in a long series of documents: *Annual Report of the Agent-General for Emigration, together with Correspondence relating to Canada and Australia,* pp. 44-65, 1839 (536-I), XXXIX; IUP Emigration 20, pp. 52-73; *Report from the Agent-General for Emigration with Correspondence,* pp. 10-21, 1840 (113), XXXIII; IUP Colonies: Australia 6, pp. 18-29; *New South Wales: Despatch relating to Immigration,* pp. 4-13, 31-41, 1840 (612), XXXIII; IUP Colonies: Australia 6, pp. 288-97, 315-25; *Correspondence relating to Land Revenue and Emigration,* pp. 3-27, 1841 (81), XVII; IUP Colonies: Australia 6, pp. 541-65; *New South Wales: Despatch from the Governor relating to Emigration,* pp. 1-19, 1841 (241), XVII; IUP Colonies: Australia 6, pp. 609-27; *New South Wales: Despatch from the Governor relating to the Introduction of Emigrants on Bounty,* pp. 2-3, 1841 Sess. 2 (10), III; IUP Colonies: Australia 6, pp. 690-1; *Correspondence between the Colonial Office and Authorities in the Colonies relating to Emigration,* pp. 1-5, 1842 (301), XXXI; IUP Emigration 21, pp. 41-5 (Stanley's despatch).

39   *Returns of the Names of Persons in the Service or Pay of the Commissioners . . .,* p. 6, 1852-53 (23), LXVIII; IUP Emigration 22, p. 448.

mechanics are generally above it; old people are useless; young children inconvenient. Idlers are mischievous in a colony; active people can generally get on at home. Single men are not desired in excess of single women, and respectable single women are not generally anxious to try the risks of a new country. People whose savings would enable them to become employers of labour instead of labourers, swell the evil which they are sent out to remedy. Lastly, the rate of contribution required by us from the emigrant himself, was a further and very operative check upon the number of applications.[40]

As applicants appeared, the Commissioners began to charter ships.[41] Owners had to agree to certain standards of construction, ventilation, manning and victualling. They received an agreed sum for every emigrant landed alive, and half for any who had died, once it had been established by investigation in the colony that all provisions of the charter-party had been complied with. Emigrants had to pay their fare to the port, equip themselves with a prescribed outfit of clothes, and produce birth and marriage certificates, proof of vaccination, and testimonials from house-holders, doctors, magistrates or clergymen.[42]

The voyage was not left to the management of master and officers alone. A Surgeon-Superintendent was engaged, who was given one-way cabin passage, ample baggage space, and a seat at the captain's table, in return for his exacting duties. He worked under a detailed code of rules, covering medical inspection and mustering before sailing, cleanliness and order at sea, education and religious services, and considerable supervision of disembarkation. He was required to keep a general journal and a medical journal. He acted as ship's doctor, maintained discipline among emigrants, but at the same time protected them against ill-treatment or neglect. On arrival, he could expect a gratuity of ten shillings per emigrant

40 *Twelfth General Report of the Colonial Land and Emigration Commissioners*, pp. 21-4, 1852 [1499], XVIII; IUP Emigration 11 (the quotation is on p. 22). The Commissioners also faced the probability that immigrants would at once participate in the gold rush instead of doing the jobs the settlers wanted done.

41 *Eleventh General Report of the Colonial Land and Emigration Commissioners*, pp. 37-40, 1851 [1383], XXII; IUP Emigration 11 shows vessels of 500 to 1,000 tons between 1849 and 1851, usually carrying two or three hundred emigrants, and taking four months to reach Sydney.

42 Regulations for 1848 may be found in *Despatches relating to Emigration to the Australian Colonies*, pp. 75-80, 1849 (593), XXXVIII; IUP Colonies: Australia 11, pp. 97-102. Each applicant had to be supported by two householders (neither of whom was to be a publican); a doctor was to certify health and vaccination; and the magistrate or clergyman was to authenticate the other signatures. The Commissioners provided bedding and utensils, which well-behaved passengers were allowed to keep at disembarkation. Men were advised to take tools. Each adult's baggage could occupy twenty cubic feet and weigh up to half a ton.

on his first or second voyage, and up to sixteen shillings for seventh and later voyages.[43] This in itself points to what became an important feature of the Commissioners' policy, the building up of an experienced corps of Surgeons. To select them was far from easy; and the Report of 1850 discusses the rival merits of naval surgeons, accustomed to imposing discipline, and of country doctors, closer to the working class and far more accustomed to handling the leading medical problems of an emigrant voyage, children's diseases and births.[44] In 1856-57, seventy-one men were employed, only one lacking previous experience and twenty with more than three previous voyages. In 1869, the last main year of their emigration operations, the Commissioners reported that eighteen of their twenty-one Surgeons had made from ten to twenty voyages.[45]

Payments of the Surgeon's gratuity, and of those to master and senior officers (a small sum per head of all landed alive), depended upon inspection at the voyage's end. The Immigration Agent at Adelaide, appointed in 1848, was required by his instructions to board arriving vessels, obtain passenger lists from Surgeons, and check them against the mustered immigrants. Having already corresponded with employers, he was to inform immigrants of the opportunities open to them. He was to take great care about the hiring of young women. He was to take certificates from the Surgeons which would determine the officers' gratuities. He was to report quickly to the Lieutenant-Governor; and the document was to contain his judgement on the Surgeon-Superintendent's conduct.[46] Regulations were soon in force in each colony, governing hiring

43   Instructions for 1839, including the need to select constables and a teacher, are in *Annual Report of the Agent-General for Emigration together with Correspondence relating to Canada and Australia*, pp. 12-29, 1839 (536-I), XXXIX; IUP Emigration 20, pp. 20-37. The importance of status is demonstrated by the writing into the great Italian emigration law of 1901 of the rule that the official equivalent to the Surgeon-Superintendent was to sit at the captain's table.

44   *Tenth General Report of the Colonial Land and Emigration Commissioners*, p. 9, 1850 [1204], XXIII; IUP Emigration 11.

45   *Eighteenth General Report of the Colonial Land and Emigration Commissioners*, pp. 19-21, 1857-58 [2395], XXIV; IUP Emigration 13; *Nineteenth General Report of the Colonial Land and Emigration Commissioners*, pp. 15-16, 1859 Sess. 2 [2555], XIV; IUP Emigration 14 (mentioning also the atempt to build up a permanent corps of matrons to supervise single women); *Thirtieth General Report of the Colonial Land and Emigration Commissioners*, p. 13, 1870 [c.196], XVII; IUP Emigration 17.

46   *Despatches relating to Emigration to the Australian Colonies*, pp. 76-8, 1849 (593), XXXVIII; IUP Colonies: Australia 11, pp. 298-300.

of immigrants, temporary free accommodation for them, and the amenities which these quarters were to contain.[47]

Quarterly or half-yearly reports from Sydney, Melbourne and other colonial ports can therefore be found in Parliamentary Papers. Comments on many vessels were merely brief and approving. That on *Bourneuf*, which arrived in September 1852, was far more detailed, treating the quality of provisions, relations between female emigrants and seamen, the conduct of matron and schoolmaster, complaints by passengers, and the difficulties experienced by the Surgeon from Scots and Irish prejudices against giving children the medicines prescribed. This report occasioned later comments by the Commissioners, based on information supplied by the Emigration Officer at Liverpool.[48] Other reports set forth an elaborate record-of misdeeds. Governor Fitzroy's despatch of 31 October 1848, for example, enclosed Agent Merewether's report from Sydney on *Subraon*, which had carried inadequate food and medical comforts, whose master had sold liquor from his private store and at high prices and had had a girl 'consistantly in his cabin', whose seamen had mingled freely with emigrant women, and whose Surgeon, though innocent of charges entered against him in the ship's log, had been guilty of conniving at officers' misconduct and had falsified his own medical journal. Earl Grey's reply enclosed the Commissioners' regrets about the Surgeon, and an explanation about selection problems. Their report sanctioned the payment of a reduced gratuity to him and the refusal of all gratuity to the ship's officers. A later report censured the shipowners for their choice of officers, and reduced the passage-money to be paid to them. Later still, the Commissioners can be found rejecting the owners' protests.[49]

---

47 Much may be found in Merewether's Report for 1848, in *Papers relating to Emigration to the Australian Colonies*, pp. 55-62, 1850 (1163), XL; IUP Colonies: Australia 11, pp. 471-8. See also several Reports of the Commissioners: the *Tenth . . .*, pp. 50-51, 1850 [1204], XXIII; IUP Emigration 11 (immigrants' chaplain at Sydney); *Thirteenth . . .*, pp. 123-4, 129-30, 1852-53 [1647], XL; IUP Emigration 12 (hiring of immigrants, and instructions to Surgeon-Superintendents on arriving in Victoria); *Fourteenth . . .*, pp. 161-7, 184-7, 1854 [1833], XXVIII; IUP Emigration 12 (reception of young women at Sydney, and accommodation at Melbourne).

48 *Papers relating to Australia 1852-53*, pp. 169-71, 185-95, 1852-53 [1627], LXVIII; IUP Colonies: Australia 17 (with the same pagination). This volume, together with Australia 11, 13 and 19, has many of the regular reports from Australian ports. The Commissioners' brief reports on more than one hundred vessels, 1847-50, appear in *Correspondence relating to Emigration to New South Wales*, pp. 84-8, 1851 (347), XL; IUP Colonies: Australia 13, pp. 186-90.

49 *Despatches relating to Emigration to the Australian Colonies*, pp. 25-9, 111-14, 1849 (593), XXXVIII; IUP Colonies: Australia 11, pp. 147-51, 233-6; *Papers relating to Emigration to the Australian Colonies*, pp. 131-6, 1850 [1163], XL; IUP Colonies: Australia 11, pp. 547-52.

Colonial reports, however, could equally be directed against the newly-arrived passengers. *Hyderabad's* company, for example, were healthy, but showed indifference and insolence when it came to taking jobs. Some absconded even after entering into written contracts; and the girls who offered themselves as servants were totally ignorant of domestic duties.[50] More complex, and well worth analysis, is the story of the Irish female orphans shipped to Australia in 1848-49 and again three years later.

At the end of February 1848, Earl Grey sent to New South Wales a despatch on a plan to send Irish girls from workhouses. In December Governor Fitzroy answered, describing the establishment of committees at Sydney and Port Phillip, and later the Agent's description of accommodation appeared in his regular report. Not long after, news came back of the bad character of emigrants in the first ship, embarrassingly named *Earl Grey*. The Surgeon wrote a violent letter about immorality on board. The local committee investigated, and although it concluded that the charges applied to no more than a third of the women, employment difficulties were soon reported. Merivale, Under-Secretary at the Colonial Office, forwarded all the documents to the Commissioners; and they in turn called on the Dublin Emigration Officer for a report. He explained to his superiors that in selecting the women he had consulted the Guardians, and the master and matron of the workhouse, and had collected certificates of approval. The Commissioners judged his explanation satisfactory, and Grey forwarded their remarks to Fitzroy. Three weeks later, he sent reports from the Irish Poor Law Board, with the Commissioners' further comments. Most of the Surgeon's allegations about selection were rebutted; but it was admitted that two of the girls had given false names, and that such a group's behaviour was likely to include very coarse language.[51] The whole episode, reinforced by problems in other shiploads, led to a clash of interests in the colony. Melbourne City Council demanded the suspension of this type of emigration, though Merewether deplored any such precipitate step. A mass meeting of Irish citizens at once took a view opposite to the Council's. Again, however, scandals, this time concerning passengers in the ships *Roman Emperor* and *Indian* arriving at Adelaide, occasioned an exchange of reports. Again the Irish Poor Law Board was brought in; and this time it criticized the South Australian

---

50 *Despatches relating to Emigration to the Australian Colonies,* pp. 10-11, 1849 (593), XXXVIII; IUP Colonies: Australia 11, pp. 132-3.

51 *Despatches relating to Emigration to the Australian Colonies,* pp. 29-30, 1849 (593), XXXVIII; IUP Colonies: Australia 11, pp. 151-2; *Papers relating to Emigration to the Australian Colonies,* pp. 1-4, 94-8, 106-26, 1850 [1163], XL; IUP Colonies: Australia 11, pp. 417-20, 510-14, 522-42.

home at which many of the girls were lodged, for failing to impose that
severe discipline which alone could offset the bad habits of early years.[52]
By the end of 1852, however, colonial opinion began to change. Victoria
especially, under the influence of the gold rush, became obsessed by the
problem of the balance of the sexes. The Commissioners concluded that
England could not produce female emigrants in the numbers required, and
recommended the resumption of Irish pauper migration. This was done,
and more complaints were soon received; but the new opinion was well
expressed in the Melbourne Immigration Agent's grudging words:

> However objectionable the system of sending out large numbers of
> young girls, totally ignorant of the domestic duties they are required to
> perform, and, generally speaking, in a deplorable state of ignorance,
> may have hitherto appeared, I am compelled to admit that the
> occurrences of the past year have worked so vast a change in the
> prospects of the colony, and threaten so complete a revulsion of her
> social system, as to render a continued stream of female emigration
> absolutely necessary for the moral welfare of the community.[53]

The Commissioners were concerned with colonies other than the
Australian, though on a much smaller scale. There was a trickle of
migration to British North America, paupers financed by their parishes.
Assisted emigration to the Cape of Good Hope essentially imitated
Australian, both as to finance and organization.[54] Much more general was
their oversight, referred to in substantial sections of their Reports, of
private or company emigration, which again imitated many features,
including Surgeon-Superintendents, of their own system. The principal
examples were the New Zealand Company, the related Canterbury and
Otago Associations, and Byrnes' emigration to Natal.[55]

---

52 *Correspondence relating to Emigration to New South Wales,* pp. 22-3, 49-50,
1851 (347), XL; IUP Colonies: Australia 13, pp. 124-5, 151-2; *Correspondence
relating to Emigration to South and Western Australia and Van Diemen's Land,*
pp. 1-4, 38-44, 52-6, 88-94, 108-12, 1851 (347-II), XL; IUP Colonies: Australia 13,
pp. 239-42, 276-82, 292-6, 238-34, 348-52.

53 *Despatches relating to Emigration to New South Wales and Victoria,* p. 87, 1854
(436), XLVI; IUP Colonies: Australia 19, p. 105.

54 Documents on the Cape of Good Hope may be found in several of the
Commissioners' Reports: *Sixth . . . ,* pp. 70-4, 1846 [706], XXIV; IUP Emigration
10; *Ninth . . . ,* pp. 70-4, 1849 [1082], XXII; IUP Emigration 11; *Eighteenth . . . ,*
pp. 222-6, 1857-58 [2395], XXIV; IUP Emigration 13.

55 John S. Marais, *The Colonization of New Zealand* (London, 1927) and Alan F.
Hattersley, *The British Settlement of Natal* (Cambridge, 1950) are excellent
monographs.

Most of the Commissioners' Reports include pages on coolie emigration. Very careful regulations were drafted, whether for free Africans, Chinese or Indians. Surgeon-Superintendents were always shipped.[56] Codes of rules were also drawn up to govern the rights and duties of workers and employers in the colonies.[57] Yet conditions could only with great difficulty be made tolerable. Often the labourers suffered from the effects of famine or disease in their home districts. Voyages, especially from India to the West Indies, were very long, and periods of storm were almost inevitable. Welfare and discipline suffered from language problems. Worse yet, as the 1871 Commission on British Guiana begins to reveal, no central authority, with nineteenth-century attitudes, finance and personnel, could hope to curb the constant attempts by planters, and their official friends in the colonies, to lengthen periods of service, discourage repatriation, cheat workers of their wages, and impose discipline as near as possible to that of slavery.[58]

The Commissioners also had the duty of advising the Secretary of State. They aided him in reaching decisions about the price of land in Australian colonies; they advised on amendments to ensure that railways could acquire the land they needed at the minimum price; they gave an opinion as to whether shipowners should be paid their half-fare for people who had died in quarantine rather than at sea; and they assembled information

---

56   All earlier authorities are now superseded by Hugh Tinker, *A New System of Slavery: the export of Indian labour overseas 1830-1920* (London, 1974). Among innumerable documents may be singled out the following items in the Commissioners' Reports: *Sixth* . . ., Appendix 13, 1846 [706], XXIV; IUP Emigration 10 (tender and charter-party); *Twentieth* . . ., Appendices 43 and 44, 1860 [2696], XXIX; IUP Emigration 14 (Calcutta and Kwantung); *Twenty-fifth* . . ., Appendix 23, 1865 [3526], XVIII; IUP Emigration 16 (Indian Act of 1864); *Thirty-second* . . ., Appendix 21, 1872 [c.562], XVI; IUP Emigration 18 (a thirty-page Indian Act). The 1865 Report, pp. 19-20, notes that surgeons experienced in the Australian emigration system were being used on the West Indies run, but that Mauritius coolie vessels had to pick up any doctor they could find in India.

57   *Thirteenth General Report of the Colonial Land and Emigration Commissioners,* Appendix 45, 1852-53 [1647], XL; IUP Emigration 12 (Mauritius); *Twenty-fifth General Report of the Colonial Land and Emigration Commissioners,* Appendices 35, 36, 37, 1865 [3526], XVIII, IUP Emigration 16 (British Guiana, Trinidad, St. Lucia).

58   *Report of the Commissioners appointed to enquire into the Treatment of Immigrants in British Guiana, and Appendices,* 1871 [c.393], [c.393-I], [c.393-II], XX; IUP Emigration 24, pp. 169-585. For this colony's labour problems, see now Alan H. Adamson, *Sugar without Slaves: The Political Economy of British Guiana, 1838-1904* (New Haven, 1973) and Michael Moohr, 'The Economic Impact of Slave Emancipation in British Guiana, 1832-1852,' *Economic History Review,* Second Series, XXV (1972), pp. 588-607.

about the as yet undeveloped Northern Australia.[59] They also executed minor policy, signing, as representatives of the Crown, leases with private persons for the export of guano from islands just ceded by the Imam of Muscat, and for the mining of coal in Labuan.[60]

The Commissioners had one further responsibility. As soon as they were appointed, they presided over the whole system of Emigration Officers and Passenger Acts, whose early development has already been outlined.

In 1842 they published a substantial report on the amendments needed in the existing law; and their proposals took account of the views both of the officers at British ports and of A. C. Buchanan at Quebec. A bill was prepared; and in the Commons Stanley brushed aside objections by wielding the expert evidence and advice.[61] Both T. F. Elliot and T. W. C. Murdoch gave evidence before the Lords' Committee on Colonization from Ireland, reviewing the history of colonial emigration and the development of the law.[62] When a new bill was brought in early in 1851, following sundry scandals, Sidney Herbert moved for a Select Committee. Almost one-third of the witnesses were connected with the Commissioners; and it was on this evidence that the government pushed legislation through.[63] Three years later, cholera and shipwrecks led John O'Connell to move for another committee, to focus upon mortality at sea. This was set up in the face of government resistance; but after Murdoch himself, nine

59 *Correspondence relating to Crown Lands and Emigration*, pp. 65-9, 1845 (267-II), XXXII; IUP Colonies, Australia 9, pp. 87-91 (New South Wales); *Twenty-fifth General Report of the Colonial Land and Emigration Commissioners*, Appendix 43, 1865 [3526], XVIII; IUP Emigration 16 (Western Australia); *Seventh General Report of the Colonial Land and Emigration Commissioners*, p. 47, 1847 [809], XXXIII; IUP Emigration 10 (railways); *Despatches relating to Emigration to New South Wales and Victoria*, pp. 139-40, 1854 (436), XLVI; IUP Colonies: Australia 19, pp. 157-8 (half-fare); *Sixth General Report of the Colonial Land and Emigration Commissioners*, Appendix 6, 1846 [706], XXIV; IUP Emigration 10 (Northern Australia).

60 *Twenty-first General Report of the Colonial Land and Emigration Commissioners*, Appendices 48, 49, 1861 [2842], XXII; IUP Emigration 14.

61 *Colonial Land and Emigration Commissioners: Report on the Necessity of Amending the Passengers Act*, 1842 [355], XXV; IUP Emigration 10, pp. 1-28. See also *Hansard*, Third Series, lx col. 76-9; and O. MacDonagh, *Pattern of Government Growth*, pp. 139-53.

62 *Report from the Select Committee of the House of Lords on Colonization from Ireland*, qq. 1-108, 565-85, 1847 (737), (737-II), VI; *First Report of . . .*, qq. 435-643, 1847-48 (415), XVII. *Second Report of . . .*, qq. 2790-2832, 1847-48 (593), XVII. The whole inquiry is printed in IUP Emigration 4 and 5.

63 *Report from the Select Committee on the Passengers' Act*, 1851 (632), XIX; IUP Emigration 6. See also *Hansard*, Third Series, cxx col. 869-72, cxxii col. 67-72; O. MacDonagh, *Pattern of Government Growth*, pp. 220-7, 244-5. For further discussion, see my Conclusion.

Emigration Officers, and other officials had testified, and the Committee's members had shown that they took drastic regulation for granted, a very comprehensive codifying bill was drafted, which in 1855 passed without debate.[64] On the other hand, the government accepted the Commissioners' view, in 1859, that no further inquiry was needed. In 1863, a further example was given of the weight attached to the experts' advice, when a further Passenger Act was passed without preceding public inquiry and without significant discussion in Parliament.[65]

It was of course through the Emigration Officers that the Commissioners established contact with people who had already begun their emigration. The complex provisions of the Passenger Acts, however, dealing as they did with rations, cooking facilities, medical care, and space, were also summed up in an Abstract to be displayed in each vessel; and some of the most important clauses appeared also in the large Contract Ticket which each passenger had to receive.[66] At an earlier stage, would-be emigrants were helped in reaching their decisions by the publication, at fairly frequent intervals from 1843, and at a modest price, of a *Colonization Circular.* By about 1870 an issue could be two hundred pages long.[67]

Such documents, supplemented by the Statutes themselves, tell us what the law said and how it came to be made. The Commissioners did not, however, conceal the difficulty of enforcement. Their Reports regularly listed prosecutions, and the sums recovered out of court by the Emigration Officers. The Select Committees of 1851 and 1854 revealed how ignorant people were exploited by runners and keepers of lodging-houses and tradesmen; how they were berthed indiscriminately on board ship; how difficult they found it to cook their food; how debilitated they became through seasickness; and how exploitation was likely to be repeated as soon as they landed at New York. It was indeed difficult to protect emigrants effectively. The Orders in Council on the conduct of the voyage were mere gestures. There could never have been enough men to permit the appointment of Surgeon-Superintendents on the North Atlantic: men could not be found to serve even as simple ship's doctors. If fraud or

64   *First and Second Reports from the Select Committee on Emigrant Ships,* 1854 (163), (349), XIII; IUP Emigration 7. O. MacDonagh, *Pattern of Government Growth,* pp. 266-76, 296-305.

65   O. MacDonagh, *Pattern of Government Growth,* pp. 313-4, 317-8.

66   The Abstract is Appendix 14 in *Eighth General Report of the Colonial Land and Emigration Commissioners,* 1847-48 [961], XXVI; IUP Emigration 10. The Contract Ticket under the 1849 Act is Appendix 6 in the *Eleventh General Report . . .,* 1851 [1383], XXII; IUP Emigration 11.

67   F. H. Hitchins, *Colonial Land and Emigration Commission,* pp. 99-104, has useful summaries. The *Circulars* themselves are to be found in the British Museum.

violence occurred at a British port, or in a vessel driven back by weather, then indeed prosecution was possible, with the Emigration Officers prosecuting, or acting as expert witnesses. For misdeeds on the high seas there was usually no redress. It was reckoned impossible to proceed under British law, for such offences, against the American vessels which made up four-fifths of the carriers of emigrants from Britain across the Atlantic in the 1850s; and unfortunately American courts were far from zealous in enforcing their own law. When, with the Civil War, British ships almost overnight came to carry half the traffic, British courts had jurisdiction beyond dispute; but the witnesses were all on the wrong side of the ocean.[68]

Most of our evidence demonstrates that the Commissioners took their duties very seriously, though their efforts did not always meet with success. In the greatest crisis they faced, however, they seem to have been overwhelmed by events, to have been guilty of some degree of lethargy before the event and some degree of complacency after it. The point can be proved by setting against the Commissioners' pronouncements on the Irish Famine emigration the detailed reports of Buchanan from Quebec. Their Seventh Report, dealing with 1846, admitted the existence of distress in Ireland; but it insisted that government regulation must remain limited, if the emigration of poor people was not to be deterred. Australian problems, indeed, seem to have remained uppermost in the Commissioners' minds. On the last day of 1846, Grey's despatch to Lord Elgin looked towards a bigger emigration to British North America, promised additional funds, and assigned army officers to help with preparations. One week earlier, Buchanan sent his report for the year, supplemented by information from A. B. Hawke at Kingston and Dr. Douglas from the quarantine establishment of Grosse Isle. Although economic prospects for immigrants were good, he noted the marked increase of deaths at sea and in hospital admissions on arrival. In February he wrote again, urging the employment of immigrants on the Quebec-Halifax railway; but Grey's despatches of the same period all had the character of a leisurely discussion of settlement upon land. In May 1847, Douglas sent in a first, brief but grim report on the opening of the new season. In rapid succession there followed reports from the Executive

68 The Order in Council is Appendix 13 in *Eighth General Report of the Colonial Land and Emigration Commissioners*, 1847-48 [961], XXVI; IUP Emigration 10. Discussion of the enforcement problem may be found in the following Reports of the Commissioners: *Twentieth . . .*, pp. 20-3, 1860 [2696], XXIX; IUP Emigration 14; *Twenty-fourth . . .*, p. 15, 1864 [3341], XVI; IUP Emigration 15; *Twenty-ninth . . .*, p. 7, 1868-69 [4159], XVII; IUP Emigration 17. The leading authority is of course O. MacDonagh, *Pattern of Government Growth*, but for much evidence about about journeys in practice see also P. Taylor, *The Distant Magnet*, chs. 7 and 8.

Council on the large expenditure needed to cope with the influx, petitions from the Assembly and from Montreal City Council appealing for regulation and aid, then Grey's consent in June to further grants. By 1 December, we find Grey lamenting the disaster, explaining to Elgin the government action taken, and enclosing a message from the Commissioners, putting the blame essentially upon uncontrollable fever carried from Ireland. Still more expenditure was sanctioned. The Eighth Report, however, seems to the modern reader to have placed curiously little emphasis upon what had occurred. The document's normal arrangement remained unbroken, so that events unprecedented in the century, and never repeated, took their place after the routine treatment of Australia and New Zealand. References to North America concentrated on the praiseworthy behaviour of officials and the terms of the new Passenger Act. The Report's flatness of tone seems remarkable; though at the same time frantic gestures of regulation were being made, including a quite unenforceable Order in Council about discipline and cleanliness among emigrants at sea.[69]

The Last Years of the Century

From the late 1850s, our documents show how one colony after another assumed responsibility for its own land and emigration policy. In 1858 South Australia appointed a selecting agent to work in Britain, and so did the Cape of Good Hope. Queensland did the same in 1865, and in 1869 and 1872 passed comprehensive Immigration Acts. When Victoria appointed a British agent in 1869, the Commissioners admitted that their shipping operations were effectively at an end.[70] Three years after this statement in their 1870 Report, the enforcement of the Passenger Acts was transferred to the Board of Trade. Five years later again, the Commission went out of existence.[71]

69   Although the Commissioners' Reports of 1847 and 1848 treat the Famine year, most of the detail is to be found in IUP Colonies: Canada 17. See especially A. C. Buchanan's long report on the year 1847 in *Papers relative to Emigration to the British Provinces of North America*, pp. 12-32, 1847-48 [964], XLVII; IUP Colonies: Canada 17, pp. 458-78. This may usefully be compared with the detailed reports on normal summers, in *Despatch Transmitting the Annual Report of the Emigration Agent*, pp. 14-21, 1844 (181), XXXV; IUP Colonies: Canada 16, pp. 834-41; and *Papers relating to Emigration to the North American Colonies*, pp. 19-22, 1852-53 [1650], LXVIII; IUP Colonies: Canada 20, pp. 491-4. Strictly there were two A. C. Buchanans, a nephew of the same name succeeding his uncle in practice from 1835 and officially from 1838: O. MacDonagh, *Pattern of Government Growth*, p. 131 note.

70   *Thirtieth General Report of the Colonial Land and Emigration Commissioners*, p. 11, 1870 [c.196], XVII; IUP Emigration 17.

71   F. H. Hitchins, *Colonial Land and Emigration Commission*, esp. pp. 83-96.

The thinning-out of public documents which resulted left statistics in a position of far greater relative prominence. The tabulation for 1882, a year of high emigration, will serve to illustrate what can be learned from these sources. A few pages of commentary precede the figures, treating such matters as the proportion of Irish in the emigration, the efforts of Canada and the Australian colonies to stimulate a flow of emigrants in their direction, the preponderance of unmarried young people among the Irish, the higher proportion of married adults among the British but the far higher number of single men than of single women. The tables show English, Scots, Irish and foreigners to each principal country of destination; cabin and steerage passengers from each port; emigration from each port to each destination; male and female numbers, conjugal condition, and children, for each national component to each destination; occupations of British, Irish and foreigners to each destination; money remitted from North America, and money recovered for emigrants by the Emigration Officers; then the origin of persons, British and foreign, arriving in Britain from overseas, and the balance of emigration over immigration; and finally, general figures are provided as far back as 1815, national origins and destinations to 1853, conjugal condition to 1877, and the proportion of British emigrants to total population to 1853.[72]

This looks substantially fuller than in the Commissioners' days; but the separately presented Irish figures reach a wholly different level. Figures are given for the years from 1851, county by county, male and female, with estimates of ratios to population; and Munster emerges with the highest figures. From 1878, emigrants are summarized by destination, including Britain. For 1882 itself, Irish emigrants, male and female, are classified port by port and month by month; then by counties with ages (infants, 1-5, then five-year groups) and sex; then by occupation and age province by province; then by destination and county of origin: Ulster is shown to lead in emigration both to Britain and Canada, Munster to other destinations, but by a small fraction Connaught has the highest ratio of emigrants to population. A separate report is made on migratory agricultural labourers; and figures are presented by ports of embarkation, by railway stations marking the beginning of journeys, then by province, county and Poor Law Union, and finally, by county and Union, stating the labourers' land-holding in acreage categories.[73]

---

72 *Emigration and Immigration (United Kingdom), Statistical Tables for 1882 with Report from the Board of Trade,* 1883 (89), LXXVI; IUP Emigration 26, pp. 275-300.

73 *Emigration from Ireland, Statistics for 1882,* 1883 [c.3489], LXXVI; IUP Emigration 26, pp. 301-12. The same volume, pp. 155-70, has *Migratory Agricultural Labourers (Ireland), Report and Table for 1882,* 1882 [c.3438], LXXIV.

Statistical tables, however, were not the only documents produced in these years. The need for reliable information continued to be recognized, and in 1886, there was set up a new institution, the Emigrants' Information Office, run by a professional from the Colonial Office under the supervision of a committee on which there was some working-class representation. This office, operating on a very modest budget, received personal calls from some five thousand would-be emigrants in the year ending 31 March 1890; it received nearly eleven thousand letters and sent out fifty thousand, much of the correspondence being with the colonies. Booklets were printed, colony by colony, to be sold at a penny; and, together with special booklets on emigration laws and professional opportunities overseas, the whole bundle could be bought for two shillings. The brief annual report noted that good employment at home was slowing down emigration. It pointed to Argentina's intense efforts to attract population, In later years, the Office can be found placing its literature in reading rooms and workingmen's clubs.[74]

Concern for abuses which survived despite the Passenger Acts prompted one more official inquiry; but this one was conducted by the Board of Trade and not by a select committee. It was a narrow investigation, but it is valuable because it occurred so early in the steamship period, when other evidence is hard to find. Details of steerage accommodation are presented; but perhaps the most interesting section is the introduction by Joseph Chamberlain, urging that the proper comparison to make is between the steerage and the crowded quarters of the working class on shore, not the refinements of middle-class life to which investigators may have been accustomed. This problem of making relevant judgements is one that faces every student of the Atlantic crossing.[75]

Wider responsibilities were never wholly forgotten. Would not the colonies provide an outlet for depressed social groups in Britain, and should not the government extend aid? In 1889 this question was studied by the select committee on Colonization, which examined more than fifty witnesses. One of them, Charles P. Lucas who managed the Emigrants' Information Office, made a statement which echoes the Commissioners' selection problems of earlier years:

74 *Report on the Emigrants' Information Office for the Year ending 31 March 1890,* 1890 [c.6064], XLIX; IUP Emigration 27, pp. 289-93. Outside the IUP series, there is a useful historical sketch of the Emigrants' Information Office, *Memorandum on the History and Functions of the Emigrants' Information Office,* 1907 [Cd. 3407], LXVII.

75 *Emigrant Accommodation on Board Atlantic Steam Ships,* 1881 [c.2995], LXXXII; IUP Emigration 25, pp. 535-614 (Chamberlain's words are on p. 535). Earlier and inadequate reports had appeared in 1873: *43 Congress 1 Session, Senate Document 23; Report on Emigrant Ships by the Sanitary Commission of the 'Lancet'.*

The people we want to get rid of is the surplus of the townspeople; the people they want in the colonies are country people. I think that the surplus in the towns a great deal comes from the country; therefore, I think, the right thing is to try and emigrate from the country districts those people who otherwise would go into the towns. We constantly had a little time back at our office men coming and saying they wanted to emigrate, and knowing that the free emigration was only for farm labourers they would say that they were farm labourers. On inquiry it would turn out that they had been farm labourers five or six years back, that they had come to London, and had become practically useless for the purpose of emigration. If they had been caught before they left the country districts, the colonies would have got what they wanted, and London would have had one surplus man the less.[76]

The committee decided against general programmes of aid, though it made certain narrow exceptions. In this period, as earlier, paupers and others were helped very little by government funds; but time and again the special problems of Scottish crofters were given sympathetic consideration. They were investigated almost as often as handloom weavers, and over a far wider span of time.[77] Philanthropic groups, meanwhile, like Dr. Barnardo's and the Salvation Army, were sending out women and children; and their schemes sometimes came under government scrutiny.[78]

At the same time, of course, the emigration of the able-bodied flowed on, with aid coming intermittently from the Australian colonies until the depression of the 1890s, and more persistently from Canada, intent on opening the prairies.[79] In all this, the Passenger Acts apart, no British policy needed to be made.

76 *Emigration from the Congested Districts: Select Committee Report,* q. 1378, 1889 (274), X; IUP Emigration 9. The Report is summarized in S. C. Johnson, *Emigration from the United Kingdom,* pp. 30-1.

77 Early examples are the *Report from the Agent-General for Emigration to the Secretary of State for the Colonies,* Appenidix, 1837-38 (388), XL; IUP Emigration 19, pp. 387-9; and *First and Second Reports of the Select Committee on Emigration,* Scotland, 1841 (182), (333), VI; IUP Emigration 3. Much later in the century, there is a family-by-family survey of such people in a settlement in Manitoba: *Crofter and Cottar Colonization in Canada, Report from H.M. Commissioners,* Appendix, 1890 [c.6067], XXVII; IUP Colonies: Canada 30, pp. 539-59.

78 Much information on destitute children, with conflicting reports, can be found in *Immigration and Colonization: First Report of the Select Committee of the Parliament of Canada,* 1875 (275), LII; IUP Colonies: Canada 28, pp. 123-54; and in the same volume, pp. 489-524, *Immigration of Pauper Children,* 1877 (263), (392), LXXI. See also S. C. Johnson, *Emigration from the United Kingdom,* chs. x, xii.

79 Parliamentary papers contain many pages on another Australian (especially Queensland) venture, the importation of Polynesians as labourers. See for example *Queensland: Correspondence relating to the Importation of South Sea Islanders,* 1867-68 (391), (496), XLVIII, 1868-69 (408), XLIII; IUP Colonies: Australia 25, pp. 443-530, 635-718.

The 1882 statistics already referred to may have served to introduce one last problem of these years. British authorities became increasingly sensitive to the growth of immigration into Britain, consisting as it did largely of Jews from eastern Europe, who settled in London and a few other large cities. The problem became related to that of working conditions in sweatshops, in the investigation of which Beatrice Webb gained her first research experience. The whole matter was studied by a select committee in 1889; and it is noteworthy that ordinary immigrants, being easily accessible, were questioned, through interpreters, in considerable numbers, along with the expected police officers, trade unionists, and representatives of Jewish charities.[80] From that date, too, special tables of figures were published year by year. In 1903 a Royal Commission took abundant evidence and received reports even from eastern Europe; and it was from this that there emerged the Aliens Act of 1905.[81]

Conclusion: Assessment of the Documents

Because the abolition of the Colonial Land and Emigration Commission brought its annual reports and related documents to an end, we know far less about emigration in the last three decades of the nineteenth century than in the three that had gone before. This is particularly unfortunate when we remember that total British emigration remained high and that new features appeared in the movement. The relationship between the volume of emigration to the United States and to the Empire fluctuated; the Irish played a much smaller part than hitherto; and, to judge from scattered evidence, British emigration to America became more industrial, more seasonal, more dominated by unaccompanied men. Official records for these years throw no direct light upon the connections between all this and the changing societies of Britain and the countries overseas, such as the Commissioners provided in earlier times.

While, however, we ought to feel admiration and gratitude for the Commissioners' massive compilations, we must not take wholly on trust everything they give us. We can see the nine volumes and the five thousand pages of reports, and masses of colonial despatches in addition. But can we

80 *Reports from Select Committees on Emigration and Immigration (Foreigners)*, 1888 (305), XI, 1890 (311), X; IUP Emigration 8.

81 A routine report is *Emigration and Immigration (United Kingdom), Statistical Tables for 1892*, pp. 37-52, 1893-94 (138), CII; IUP Emigration 27, pp. 625-40. See also the huge Report of the Royal Commission on Alien Immigration, 1903 [Cd. 1741], [Cd. 1742], [Cd. 1741-I], [Cd. 1743], IX. The best secondary authorities are Lloyd P. Gartner, *The Jewish Immigrant in England 1870-1914* (London, 1960) and John A. Garrard, *The English and Immigration: a Comparative Study of the Jewish Influx, 1880-1910* (London, 1971).

rely on this for statistical accuracy? Does it reflect fairly the diversity of opinions and interests involved? Does it reproduce all or most of the original working papers generated by the British and colonial administrative systems? Were there still areas of human activity, relevant to emigration, with which officials concerned themselves little if at all?

Figures, certainly, should not be accepted without question, though we have to acknowledge that we may never be able to improve upon them. Most scholars agree that, for much of the nineteenth century, emigration totals collected by governments fell short of the true figures. Record-keeping at seaports was casual; opportunities for slipping aboard late, and at unauthorized places, abounded; and since Americans were equally careless, especially at the Canadian border, it is seldom possible to feel confidence in checking from figures kept on that side of the Atlantic. Not until 1853 did British statistics distinguish between countries of origin of emigrants, and American figures were vague at least as late. It is never possible to tell the number of Irish who migrated to America after an intermediate stay in England, nor how many people landed in Canada, followed better opportunities south of the border, then later drifted north.[82]

For any assessment of causes of emigration, it is obviously important to know emigrants' occupations. Did people move in response to the decay of certain industries or certain processes, to the downward swing of the business cycle, or to short-term disruption of a local industry by a strike? Did they travel with seasonal opportunities in mind? Did they intend changing occupations, and if so, did they accomplish what they planned? From the 1850s, much information is tabulated on both sides of the Atlantic, but the detail is always less than we need. Although, for example, in British statistics occupations are stated for emigrants to each principal destination overseas, we cannot distinguish a handloom from a powerloom weaver, one kind of miner from another, wage-earners in large enterprises from more or less independent craftsmen. The category 'labourer' calls for especially close scrutiny. There is nothing intrinsically improbable in the emigration of high proportions of such people, often half of all gainfully employed in a year; yet at the one point known to me, at which an independent source of information exists, the official figure falls apart. The tabulations were based upon the passenger lists; and these were compiled by people overworked at other tasks in agents' offices or on board. Confronted with hundreds of emigrants a day, all dressed in working clothes, they were prone to write 'labourer' at the head of a

82 Marcus L. Hansen, *The Mingling of the Canadian and American Peoples* (New Haven, 1940); and, more statistical, Leon C. Truesdell, *The Canadian-born in the United States* (New Haven, 1943).

column, then scrawl a series of ditto marks underneath, against each man's name. Some of these ships, however, carried Mormon converts; the Church kept its own ledgers; and unlike shipowners or governments, its leaders took a deep interest in occupations for the purpose of planning economic growth, by more or less directed labour, in Utah. When their lists can be examined, it is found that the very same passengers are given a variety of occupations, many of them skilled.[83] For other vessels, to be sure, there is no proof that the same thing occurred, and accuracy may have improved in later years; but suspicion must remain.

Our problems are made worse because there is nothing in the British, as distinct from the Irish, figures to show emigrants' geographical origins, even down to county level. So we cannot say whether miners came from Northumberland or South Wales, nor spinners from Lancashire or Renfrew, nor farm labourers from an area of high wages or of low; and it must be confessed with shame that more is known of such matters (despite all inaccuracies and evasions), not merely in Sweden, but in southern Italy or in the Hapsburg Empire. British local figures in anything like useful series exist, in fact, only for some proportions of four categories of people: Mormon converts, assisted paupers, government-assisted emigrants to Australia, and transported convicts.[84] A very recent piece of research has, indeed, somewhat extended our knowledge. By using the few thousand names in passenger lists whose compilers included more detail than the law required, Dr. Erickson has been able to show the remarkably high proportion of labourers, miners and building workers in the emigration to the United States in the 1880s; the low proportion of skilled workers from modern manufacturing industries, and of railway workers; and the over-representation of big towns and of industrial counties with high wages. She suggests that unemployment, especially in construction, was shaking loose people who had only recently arrived from the

---

83 My discovery was made while using, for my *Expectations Westward: the Mormons and the Emigration of their British Converts in the Nineteenth Century* (Edinburgh, 1965), the Latter-day Saints' Church Shipping Books in the Church Historian's Library, Salt Lake City, after having read passenger lists of some of the same vessels, from New Orleans and New York, on microfilm supplied by the National Archives, Washington.

84 *Return from the Colonies relating to the Application of Land Rvenues to Emigration, 1837-47,* following p. 14, 1847-48 (345), XLVII; IUP Emigration 22, following p. 314 (Poor Law emigrants, county by county); *Returns of the Number of Emigrants and the Expenses incurred by them, 1846-50,* following p. 2, 1851 (680), XL; IUP Emigration 22, following p. 412 (Government emigrants, county by county); Ross Duncan, 'Case Studies in Emigration: Cornwall, Gloucestershire and New South Wales, 1875-1866', *Economic History Review,* Second Series, XVI, pp. 272-89; A. G. L. Shaw, *Convicts and Colonies,* chs. 7 and 8; P. A. M. Taylor, *Expectations Westward,* esp. pp. 248-9.

countryside.[85] That all this is typical is likely enough; but the evidence is on a very small scale.

Reliability involves much more than the accuracy of figures. In particular, do the numerous and lengthy official inquiries present a true picture of events and a balanced reflection of opinions; and if they do not, is this due to mere error or to some intentional bias? Any student of American politics knows how an investigation may be distorted by the selection of witnesses and by the way in which they are treated when they appear; and examples of inquiries in the Parliamentary Papers must be looked at with care.

The select committees which sat in 1826 and 1827 were made up of what looks like a fair selection of Members of Parliament. They examined about one hundred witnesses. It is known that they were questioned because they happened to be in London, not because they were necessarily the best representatives of a part of Britain or of a colony; but proportions, roughly, of one-quarter Irish landowners, about half British gentry, businessmen and even a handful of workers, a dozen colonial officials, and some twenty settlers, all this gives an impression of serious-minded honesty. Yet the committee framed questions that permitted only a narrow range of reply; and it is impossible to escape the conclusion that they sought a result already determined by Wilmot-Horton and those who thought like him.[86] The 1836 committee on the Disposal of Lands in the British Colonies displayed a rather similar spirit, though the method was different. It examined only eleven witnesses, four of whom were closely connected with the South Australian venture. Edward Gibbon Wakefield and Robert Torrens took up nearly five days of the proceedings; Wakefield alone answered about one-quarter of all the questions the Committee put; and some of his answers occupy a third or even a half of a page of print. One almost visualizes a docile class feeding questions to a strong-willed tutor, and eliciting from him short expositions of pure doctrine.[87] Investigations, on the other hand, could be warped, not by the will of their sponsors, but by the nature of the circumstances leading to their establishment. The Board of Trade inquiry of 1881, into emigrant steamships on the North Atlantic, was defective in that no emigrant was ever questioned, and no investigator travelled further than Queenstown. It

---

85   Charlotte Erickson, 'Who were the English and Scots Emigrants to the United States in the late Nineteenth Century?' in D. V. Glass and R. Revelle, *Population and Social Change* (London, 1972).

86   *Report from the Select Committee on Emigration from the United Kingdom,* 1826 (404), IV; *First, Second and Third Reports from . . .,* 1826-27 (88), (237), (550), V; IUP Emigration 1 and 2. See the comments in H. J. M. Johnston, *British Emigration Policy,* ch. vi.

87   The evidence is in 1836 (512), XI; IUP Colonies: General 2, pp. 185-451.

failed also, however, because its narrow emphasis on washrooms, berthing, and presence or absence of watchmen at night was occasioned by its having to respond to sensational allegations which had stressed sexual misconduct in the ships.[88]

Not all inquiries had these characteristics. The Lords' Committee on Colonization from Ireland seems to have tried to secure a comprehensive range of views from Australia and British North America, from Irish landowners, from officials and others concerned with emigration, even from a New York merchant who could give information about conditions at that port. Although no emigrants were examined, Stephen de Vere's account of steerage life was put in evidence, as were eleven pages of Irish emigrant letters.[89] The 1854 Committee on Emigrant Ships, though established to report on the causes of mortality at sea, ranged widely in its questioning. Among its witnesses were shipowners, a doctor who had made Atlantic crossings, a gentleman who claimed to have observed life in the steerage, and one Irish emigrant whose vessel had been driven by storm damage back to port. Officials of course took the lead, especially T. W. C. Murdoch, the senior Commissioner.[90] Because of its relevance and comprehensiveness, the 1851 Committee on the Passengers' Acts has been singled out for more detailed study.

The first point to be considered is the Committee's treatment of witnesses. Leading questions, to be sure, were a common feature of the proceedings, for this was not a court of law. The chairman, Sidney Herbert, 'asked' the senior Commissioner T. W. C. Murdoch:

It has been proposed to us that there should be a central booking-office, in which the passages should be secured by the Government officer, and every passenger coming to be booked should of necessity go by the next ship that sails or by the first ship standing on the list: that would at once establish a complete monopoly in favour of certain

---

88   *Emigrant Accommodation on Board Atlantic Steam Ships*, 1881 [c.2995], LXXXII; IUP Emigration 25, pp. 535-614.

89   *First Report from the Select Committee of the House of Lords on Colonization from Ireland*, q. 461 (De Vere's letter) 1847-48 (415) XVII; *Third Report of . . .*, Appendix, pp. 122-32 (emigrants' letters), 1849 (86), XI; both in IUP Emigration 5. See also Vere Foster's letter in *Emigrant Ship 'Washington': Correspondence relating to the Treatment of Passengers*, pp. 1-7, 1851 (198), XL; IUP Emigration 22, pp. 401-7.

90   *First and Second Reports from the Select Committee on Emigrant Ships*, 1854 (163), (349), XIII; IUP Emigration 7 (the Questions are numbered continuously). Murdoch's evidence is in qq. 1-681, 3714-3885; Dr. O'Doherty's, qq. 682-901; Mr. Delaney Finch's, qq. 2068-2394; and John Ryan's qq. 3886-4066.

shipowners probably, and would place the whole thing at the discretion of the Government officer, and of course lay him open to accusations of favouritism, and so on, in the selection of ships, would it not? (q. 7175)

To this Murdoch replied: 'I think the plan is wrong in principle and impossible in practice.' Instances as glaring as this are few; and most of them reflect the members' deep concern for the principle of private enterprise. Henley asked the secretary of the Birkenhead Dock Company: 'You would propose, in fact, that these men should be treated like sheep, which are taken to be sold in a particular market; you would say that they could not be driven to any other place than this particular pen, and that there the shipowners might go and bid for them?' (q. 1584). Herbert asked Sir George Stephen: 'Do you consider that a man having no property or means ought to be deprived of his free agency?' (q. 4152). Apart from this, it is impossible to find any instances of serious pressure upon witnesses, who in any case were men well able to maintain their position. Certainly the Committee did nothing to prevent some from being taciturn and some verbose: contrast Captain Patey and Sir George Stephen.

It is of course true that the Committee did not conduct its investigation according to a perfectly coherent and systematic plan. Of the fifteen members, only four or five played a prominent part in the questioning. Herbert, who had proposed the inquiry, who was the chairman, and who was the only man to have sat in a cabinet, quite naturally took the lead. No member seems to have specialized in any particular topic. Nor was the order of business carefully planned: witnesses from the Clyde were taken one after another, but on London conditions Lean's evidence was widely separated from Bowler's. Quite properly, Liverpool evidence was given overwhelming prominence. On the other hand, only two witnesses gave first-hand information about conditions emigrants faced on arrival in North America. Murdoch's two blocks of evidence, about eight hundred answers in all, formed, as it were, a frame for the inquiry, laying the groundwork and then clearing up the Committee's later difficulties when the whole body of evidence was available to them and to himself.

Taken as a whole, the seven weeks of sessions, and the more than seven thousand questions and answers, covered the ground fully enough. The problem of how to defeat runners was thoroughly discussed. The inadequacy of medical inspection was exposed, as well as the steady campaign to ship defective provisions. The improper method of assigning berths was uncovered, though witnesses disagreed as to the extent to which clerks took bribes. The confusion resulting from individual cooking by emigrants was vividly described. The difficulty of obtaining competent men as surgeons in emigrant ships was clearly stated. Several methods of securing cleanliness and order at sea were discussed; and while it was seen to be difficult to introduce on to the North Atlantic the Australian system of surgeon-superintendents, it was admitted (q. 4249) that anyone assigned to such a job should be 'a man in authority, and in such a position in society as to mess at the captain's table, and so ensure a degree of respect and obedience from the passengers' as well as being able to exert influence over the ship's officers. From time to time, beneath the vigorous arguments of reformers, can be heard the resigned voices of those who have lived with the problems only too long. Captain Patey remarked (q. 5372): 'A man going to sea is very often sea-sick . . . a man sleeps the greater part of his voyage, and has little or nothing to do, and I think that the provisions supplied are sufficient.' Answering questions about 'indecency' on board, the passenger broker Tapscott remarked (q. 2564): 'On board ship people become accustomed to things, and do not expect to find them the same as they do on shore; matters cannot be arranged on board ship as they are on shore.'

The committee's report contained a mixture of reforming proposals and free-enterprise pronouncements. It was enough, however, when backed by the evidence and by separate revelations from American sources that showed one witness, Lieutenant Hodder, to have been less than frank in his answers, to lead to a very comprehensive statute.[91]

It must also be asked whether a fair range of interests is represented in documents from the colonies. The committees of the New South Wales Legislative Council, which took evidence on immigration and related topics in several years between 1835 and 1843, usually heard officials, landowners (who were often justices of the peace), Sydney merchants, and in 1843 a builder, a foreman, and several artisans. Working-class representation was exceptional, though this is not surprising at such a date; and very seldom were people heard who had travelled with immigrants. The committees, of course, were far more concerned with the development of the colonial economy than with conditions during the voyage; and it was not unreasonable that they should hear a preponderance of landed settlers, as the principal employers of labour, with a few officials to testify on the need for men on the public works. Until the controversy between squatters and small farmers broke out, conflicts of interest within New

91 *Report from the Select Committee on the Passengers' Act,* 1851 (632), XIX; IUP migration 6. See also O. MacDonagh, *Pattern of Government Growth,* esp. 224-5.

South Wales were neither acute nor varied; and our documents may be judged to have been representative enough.[92]

If such is the reliability of the evidence, what proportion do the documents bear to the total information about emigration that exists?

Editors responsible for a publishing project as gigantic as the one of which the Emigration set forms part faced a task of extraordinary complexity; and it is not to be expected that every researcher will approve every one of their decisions. What must be stated with emphasis, however, is that remarkably little material relevant to the subject has been lost. The 1849 report by Captain Denham, thirty-four pages long, on conditions on board steamships between Ireland and Liverpool, has been omitted. So has the report of an interdepartmental inquiry, in 1882, about Scandinavians crossing the North Sea to Hull on their way to Liverpool and the Atlantic steamships.[93] That is all; for it is no fault of the editors that they could not supplement their documents, beginning in 1889, dealing with foreigners settling in Britain, with the big report of the Royal Commission on Alien Immigrants, for this was published not in the nineteenth century but in 1903.[94]

In the days of the Colonial Land and Emigration Commissioners, a very high proportion of the working papers of governmental agencies was put

92 Six long instalments of such proceedings can be found: for 1835, *Emigration: Correspondence between the Secretary of State and the Governors of the Australian Colonies*, pp. 4-55, 1837 (358), XLIII, IUP Colonies: Australia 5, pp. 92-143; for 1837, *Canada and Australia: Correspondence and a Report relating to Emigration to those Colonies*, pp. 31-62, 1837-38 (389), XL; IUP Emigration 19, pp. 433-64; for 1839, *New South Wales: Despatch relating to Immigration*, pp. 4-54, 1840 (612), XXXIII; IUP Colonies: Australia 6, pp. 288-338; for 1840, *New South Wales: Despatches from the Governor relating to Emigration*, pp. 2-19, 1841 (241), XVII; IUP Colonies: Australia 6, pp. 610-27; for 1841, *Correspondence between the Colonial Office and the Authorities in the Colonies relating to Emigration*, pp. 38-111, 121-67 (New South Wales and Van Diemen's Land respectively) 1842 (301) XXXI; IUP Emigration 21, pp. 78-151, 161-207; and for 1843, *New South Wales: Correspondence relating to the Depressed State of the Colony and to Emigration*, pp. 116-77, 1844 (505), XXXV; IUP Colonies: Australia 7, pp. 556-617.

93 *Report by Captain Denham on Passenger Accommodation in Steamers between Ireland and Liverpool*, 1849 (339), LI; *Reports received by the Board of Trade and the Local Government Board relating to the Transit of Scandinavian Emigrants through the Port of Hull*, 1882 (279), LXII. One may also regret the absence of the Devon Commission Report, *Royal Commission on the Law and Practice ... Occupation of Land in Ireland*, 1845 (605), (606), XIX, (616), XX, (657), XXI, (672), XXII, which would have thrown much light upon pre-famine conditions in Ireland as the background of emigration.

94 See note 81 above. The interesting study of American immigration depots, *Reports to the Board of Trade by Messrs. Schloss and Burnett on U.S. Legislation and Practice as to Alien Immigrants* (c.7113], 1893-94 LXXI; IUP Area Studies: United States 47, pp. 205-596.

into print. Of course there are manuscript collections of vast bulk dealing with colonial affairs, as anyone can see who consults the bibliographies in Macdonald's monographs on Canada, Roberts' on Australian land settlement, or Hartwell's on Van Diemen's Land.[95] On emigration strictly defined, however, we need regret the absence, from the original Parliamentary Papers and therefore from the present reprint edition, of no more than three classes of papers. The first is the series of reports from the Emigration Officers to the Commissioners or their predecessors, out of which so much policy-making emerged: Lieutenant Low sent in thirty such reports from Liverpool in 1833 and 1834 alone. Second, we seldom gain any impression of the instructions the Commissioners sent down to the ports, sometimes, as MacDonagh shows, warning them against exceeding their authority, more often heaping new duties upon them and encouraging them to exercise a broad discretion. Finally, we lack the letters to the Commissioners from shipowners, making representations against proposed clauses in Passenger Acts, or protesting after the event.[96] The effect of all this is to give the researcher the results of policy-making, while concealing much of the local and personal detail, much of the clash of interests, and much of the argument within organizations, that lay behind it. Those writers who have looked behind the printed sources relating to the Passenger Acts, therefore, have arrived at a judgement notably more pessimistic than have those content to read printed reports and committee evidence alone; for these have something of a smoothing effect upon the harshness of reality.[97]

Even if manuscripts are added to the parliamentary papers, however, it remains true that the British government was not equally interested in all aspects of emigration. Responsibilities were defined by statute and were exercised within a given administrative framework; and no officials went beyond the system out of prophetic insight into the needs of researchers in 1976. Limitations in the statistics have already been exposed. Little

95   N. Macdonald, *Canada 1763-1841*, and *Canada: Immigration and Colonization 1841-1903* (Aberdeen, 1966); S. H. Roberts, *History of Australian Land Settlement;* R. M. Hartwell, *Economic Development of Van Diemen's Land.*

96   O. MacDonagh, *Pattern of Government Growth,* esp. 94 note, 109 note, 138-9, 153-5, 158-60, 203, 242. MacDonagh shows, too, pp. 257-65, that there was much interdepartmental correspondence which was never printed. A rare item in Parliamentary Papers is a set of instructions to Emigration Officers about the enforcement of the 1852 Passenger Act, *Returns relating to Emigration Officers and Medical Inspectors,* pp. 4-32, 1854 (255), XLVI; IUP Emigration 23, pp. 12-40.

97   In addition to MacDonagh, *Pattern of Government Growth,* see Terry Coleman, *Passage to America* (London, 1972). My own treatment in *The Distant Magnet,* ch. 7, could be accused of minimizing the horrors; but I was dealing with a much wider period than 1846-55, and with Germans and Scandinavians, not all of whom sailed in overcrowded ships, not just with Irish.

attention was paid to white migration from one colony to another, except when a situation was as turbulent as the Victoria gold rush.[98]   Even more important, governmental agencies did not need to concern themselves much with the United States, though this was usually the most important emigration field. Fortunately, the researcher has at his disposal abundant (though not indeed perfect) sources from the American side. The Immigration Commission, it is true, worked in the twentieth century; but we have a highly interesting series of investigations either side of 1890, and a volume of the Industrial Commission's evidence in 1899.[99]

Even for British colonies, official documents neglect the fate of most emigrants once they had disembarked and passed through the ports. Apart from Hawke in Upper Canada, no official played, in the interior, the role of Buchanan in Quebec, Pinnock and Merewether at Sydney.[100] Moreover, governmental agencies in Britain were likely to take less interest in economic and social affairs (which after all were colonial responsibilities or matters for private initiative alone) than in administration and constitutional growth. Parliamentary papers do not wholly lack information about rural life in the colonies; but they are far more comprehensive about land-law, claims to self-government, or relations between New Zealand's white settlers and the Maories.

By definition, after all, parliamentary papers are the products of a government. It follows, therefore, that the researcher must supplement them with a wide range of material derived from more private sources. Newspapers, business records, and local histories may yield a little on the elusive British background of emigration. Diaries and letters, however scarce, help us to understand conditions at sea.[101] Advertising material can be found in the publications of land companies, railways, shipping lines,

---

98   Some such figures can be found in three of the Colonial Land and Emigration Commissioners' Reports: *Twelfth . . .*, pp. 35, 38, 139, 1852 [1499], XVIII; IUP Emigration 11; *Thirteenth . . .*, pp. 35, 38, 80, 1852-53 [1647], XL; IUP Emigration 12; *Fifteenth . . .*, p. 127, 1854-55 [1953], XVII; IUP Emigration 12.

99   *50 Congress 1 Session, House Miscellaneous Document 572*, Select Committee on Contract Labor; *51 Congress 2 Session, House Report 3472*, Select Committee on Immigration and Naturalization; *52 Congress 1 Session, House Executive Document 235*, Reports . . . Causes . . . Immigration to the United States; *52 Congress 1 Session, House Miscellaneous Documents 19 and 20*, Special Consular Reports; *52 Congress 1 Session, House Report 2090*, Joint Committee on Ellis Island; *Reports of Industrial Commission*, XV.

100   Examples of his work are in *Emigration, North America and New South Wales*, pp. 25-7, 1843 (109), XXXIV; IUP Colonies: Canada 16, pp. 605-7; *Papers relative to Emigration to the British Provinces of North America*, pp. 28-30, 1847 [777], XXXIX; IUP Colonies: Canada 17, pp. 72-4.

101   P. Taylor, *The Distant Magnet*, chs. 7 and 8.

colonial governments, and American states.[102] As for emigrants after their arrival overseas, travellers' narratives, county histories, newspapers, early social surveys, and censuses are all likely to be needed, as well as the trade and trade-union press used so skilfully by Rowland Berthoff.[103]

It is a fortunate accident that, while this Commentary was being prepared, there appeared a book pioneering in the scholarly use of private records for the study of British emigration. Dr. Erickson has used as her base a collection of letters which linked people in the United States with those who stayed at home. These, to be sure, make up no more than a tiny fraction of all the letters ever written, and no one can guarantee that they are typical. Yet they exist; and by ingenuity they may be forced to reveal much, both as to facts and attitudes. When a few individual letter-writers are known, they can be traced on both sides of the Atlantic. By doing all this, Dr. Erickson has produced an important analysis of the experience of emigrants who moved from farm life to farm life, from industry to agriculture, from factory work to factory work, or from manual to white-collar employment, with their family links, their sources of funds, their attitudes to Americans around them, all made clear.[104]

This may be the most fruitful line of advance for research into British emigration; but such work can never be complete, and much that we should like to discover will undoubtedly remain for ever unknown. The adventurous researcher, however, will continue to respond to the excitement of the history of several countries, several levels of technology, varied types of government policy, and above all the experiences of the knowable fraction of millions of people; and as he goes about his task with obstinacy, zeal and disciplined imagination, he will find the parliamentary papers, for all their defects, a massive base.

102   Wilbur S. Shepperson, *British Emigration to North America: Projects and Opinions in the Early Victorian Period* (Oxford, 1957); P. Taylor, *The Distant Magnet,* ch. 4 (with full references).

103   Rowland T. Berthoff, *British Immigrants in Industrial America* (Cambridge, Mass., 1952).

104   C. Erickson, *Invisible Immigrants.*

The Documents

The gradual definition of an organized emigration policy by members of Select Committees of the House of Commons and its practical implementation by the Colonial Land and Emigration Commissioners provide centralizing themes for the material in these papers. The growing strength and organization of the emigration movement, the promotion of emigration and protection of emigrants, an emerging and clearly defined emigration policy and the political and practical problems encountered are accurately recorded. Extensive information is presented on the reasons for large-scale emigration, on the conditions of emigrants and their prospects abroad, as well as on the attitudes and approaches of colonial legislatures and foreign powers to emigration.

Emigration in the nineteenth century was a phenomenon perhaps as important in its effects as the Industrial Revolution. The British parliamentary papers contain a comprehensive documentation of this movement. Emigration from the United Kingdom created the labour forces of the great productive countries of the colonial world, the United States, Canada, Australia and South Africa. In the earlier years of the century emigration was a disorganized force lacking purpose and planning. But as the century developed, control, finance and an overall sense of purpose was injected by the British Government.

The Irish University Press Emigration set consists of twenty-eight volumes organized in three distinct but complementary sections arranged in chronological order. The first section (volumes 1-9) contains select committee reports on emigration and colonization from the United Kingdom. Section two (volumes 10-18) comprises the reports of the Colonial Land and Emigration Commissioners whose function was to survey the settling of colonists abroad, to compile and assess statistics, to advise on technical problems associated with emigration and to control intercolonial emigration and emigration from foreign countries to the colonies. The third section (volumes 19-28) includes the remaining reports and correspondence, as well as the general papers, despatches and statistical returns relating to emigration.

Emigration 1   Report from the select committee on emigration from the United Kingdom, with minutes of evidence, appendix and index, 1826. (384 pp. 2 coloured maps, 1 folding)

By the 1820s, pressure of population and economic distress were especially acute in Ireland and the Highlands of Scotland; and the select committee had to consider how far emigration could be the remedy. It decided to recommend that emigration should not be state-aided, and that any loans given to emigrants should carry interest; but it recognized that abundant evidence existed for the economic benefits of advance preparations for settlers' farming, and of loans to help them buy a workable acreage. Consideration was given to a model farm scheme in Colombia. Naturally the committee paid particular attention to Ireland, where landlords might be encouraged to pay for their tenants' passage to America in order to clear their estates for more rational use.

Original reference
1826   (404) IV   Emigration, Sel. Cttee. Rep., mins. of ev., etc.

Emigration 2   First, second and third reports from the select committee on emigration from the United Kingdom, with minutes of evidence, appendix and index, 1826-27. (892 pp. 6 folding maps, 3 coloured)

Unemployment and poverty were severe among traditionally skilled workers who had been displaced by machinery. Wages had fallen below subsistence level in some places; the Poor Law could not fully alleviate the distress; and people therefore wished to emigrate. Many Irish who could not afford to reach America settled instead in Scotland or the North of England, still further threatening wages there.

The committee wished to encourage emigration, but refused to take the initiative away from parish organizations or emigration societies. The most it would do was recommend an Exchequer grant of £50,000 to supplement local resources.

Evidence was taken from shipowners, representatives of emigration societies, Poor Law authorities, and emigrants; and the extent of distress was clearly to be seen. Malthus, called as a witness, argued that emigration from Ireland to England and Scotland should be stopped, and that Irish landlords should encourage tenants to emigrate to America. Appendices present returns of emigration in the past, an estimate of emigration expenses, details of poverty, and memorials from groups of destitute artisans.

Original references

1826-27 (88) V	Emigration from the United Kingdom, Sel. Cttee. 1st Rep.
(237)	Emigration from the United Kingdom, Sel. Cttee. 2nd. Rep., mins. of ev.
(550)	Emigration from the United Kingdom, Sel. Cttee 3rd Rep., mins of ev., appendix, index.

Emigration 3 First and second reports from the select committee on emigration, Scotland, with minutes of evidence, appendices and index, 1841. (336 pp.)

The select committee concluded that there was an excess of between 45,000 and 80,000 people in the Highlands and Hebrides, many of whom would have starved during some years but for government aid. The solution recommended was a large emigration, with the government paying passage-money and employing a high proportion of the men on colonial public works.

Original references
1841	(182) VI	Emigration, Scotland, Sel. Cttee. Rep., mins. of ev., etc.
	(333)	Emigration, Scotland, Sel. Cttee. Rep., mins. of ev., etc.

Emigration 4 Report from the select committee of the House of Lords on colonization from Ireland, with minutes of evidence, appendix and index, 1847. (864 pp. 5 folding maps, 2 coloured)

Many Irish emigrants had been successful in North America or Australia. This in turn had led to further emigration as savings were sent back as remittances to families. Faced with the Great Famine, the Lords committee studied documentary evidence from inquiries of the past three decades into Irish poverty and emigration, as well as hearing witnesses both on Irish conditions and on the demand for labour in British colonies. The evidence showed that Irish poverty had outstripped the capacity of the local rates to relieve; and the committee therefore wished to see emigration planned in such a way as to develop colonial resources through rural settlement.

Original references
1847	(737) VI	Colonization from Ireland, Sel. Cttee. HL. Rep., mins. of ev.
	(737-II)	Colonization from Ireland, Sel. Cttee. HL. app. and index.

Emigration 5 First, second and third reports from the select committee of the House of Lords on colonization from Ireland, with minutes of evidence, appendix and index, 1847-49. (612 pp. 5 folding maps, 4 coloured)

This volume contains no further report of any more than a procedural kind; but there is much additional evidence on conditions in Canada,

South Africa, Australia, New Zealand and the United States. The committee examined the process by which new immigrants were absorbed into the overseas countries. Much evidence, too, was presented on the value to the home country of expanding trade with the new lands. Appendices are exceptionally full, and include both a crude census of New South Wales and a tabulation, by poor-law unions, of the numbers of Ireland's inhabitants holding different acreages of land.

Original references

1847-48 (415) XVII	Colonization from Ireland, Sel. Cttee. HL. 1st Rep., mins. of ev.
(593)	Colonization from Ireland, Sel. Cttee. HL. 2nd Rep., mins. of ev.
1849 (86) XI	Colonization from Ireland, HL. 3rd Rep., app. and index.

Emigration 6 Report from the select committee on the Passengers' Act with proceedings, minutes of evidence, appendix and index, 1851. (1,004 pp.)

Emigration increased rapidly during the 1840s, and by the end of the decade was running at a quarter of a million a year. Virtually all of these people were making their own private plans for the journey and for finding work, especially in America. In so doing, they were exposed to victimization, and into this it was the Committee's task to inquire. Since no British authorities could control the emigrants' fate after disembarkation, it was to the regulation of ports and ships that the committee directed its attention.

The emphasis was always upon North American emigration. Witnesses were mostly Emigration Officers or other government agents, and people connected with the shipping business. From the committee's recommendations on food, sanitary conditions, separation of the sexes, and many other matters, the Passenger Act of 1852 emerged.

Original reference

1851 (632) XIX	Passengers' Act. Sel. Cttee. Rep., mins. of ev., etc.

Emigration 7 First and second reports from the select committee on emigrant ships with proceedings, minutes of evidence, appendix and index, 1854. (448 pp. 3 plans, 2 folding)

The committee was established because of loss of life in emigrant ships both from shipwreck and disease; and its duty was to apportion blame and recommend precautions for the future. Taking evidence from officials, a ship's doctor, and even one emigrant, the committee found that the provisions of the 1852 Act had been widely disregarded. Several ships had left port with passengers suffering from cholera. Vessels were still unseaworthy, overcrowded and under-manned, equipped with utterly inadequate lifeboats and far too few water-closets. Vessels carrying iron cargoes were mentioned as the most dangerous of all. Despite the widespread shipowner's view that further regulation would reduce profits or raise fares beyond the capacity of the poorer emigrants to pay, the committee recommended new instalments of reform.

Original references

| 1854 | (163) XIII | Emigrant ships, Sel. Cttee. 1st Rep., mins. of ev., etc. |
| | (349) | Emigrant ships, Sel. Cttee. 2nd Rep., mins. of ev., etc. |

Emigration 8 Reports from the select committees on emigration and immigration (foreigners) with proceedings, minutes of evidence, appendices and indices, 1888-89. (520 pp.)

Towards the end of the nineteenth century, emigration from eastern Europe became large. Some of these people, Russian Jews especially, passed through Britain on their way to the United States, others remained to work in London's East End or in the crowded districts of provincial cities. These immigrants, many of them skilled workers, seemed to threaten wages in such trades as shoemaking and tailoring. Their clustering in communities also caused many British observers deep concern.

After taking evidence from British artisans' representatives (including the labour leader Keir Hardie), from sanitary, education and police officers, and from many of the newcomers, the committee recommended the keeping of far more exact statistics than the 1881 census had been found to contain; and tables of figures were in fact published in each subsequent year. While it recommmended no immediate restrictions, the possible need for future measures was seen, and American experience was cited.

Original references

| 1888 | (305) XI | Emigration and immigration (foreigners), Sel. Cttee. Rep., mins. of ev., etc. |
| 1889 | (311) X | Emigration and immigration (foreigners), Sel. Cttee. Rep., mins. of ev., etc. |

Emigration 9   Reports from select committees on colonization with minutes of evidence, appendices and indices, 1889-91. (992 pp.)

The select committees of 1889, 1890 and 1890-91 were set up to examine various schemes proposed to the government to facilitate emigration from the congested districts of Great Britain to the British colonies or elsewhere. They investigated, in addition, the desirability of further promoting emigration and in what direction. The evidence heard by the first two committees was considered by the 1890-91 committee in preparing their report. One of the principal areas of investigation was the emigration of Scottish crofters and cottars to Canada. The committee expressed satisfaction with the prevailing conditions for such emigrants and urged an increase of emigration to Canada from Scotland to relieve the distress among the crofters. Comparisons were made by the committee between Scottish and Irish emigration. The outcome was a strong recommendation for the extension of the Land and Congested Districts (Ireland) Bill provisions to Scotland. The reconstruction of the Crofter Colonization Board was also proposed. Other matters reported on by the committee were the Emigrants' Information Office instituted in 1886, emigration to New Zealand, Australia and other colonies, and the ability of emigrants to settle and earn a livelihood in the colonies.

Original references

1889	(274) X	Colonization, Sel. Cttee. Rep., mins. of ev., etc.
1890	(354) XII	Colonization, Sel. Cttee. Rep., mins. of ev., etc.
1890-91	(125) XI	Colonization, Sel. Cttee. Rep., mins. of ev., etc.

Emigration 10   General reports of the colonial land and emigration commissioners with appendices, 1842-48. (528 pp.)

The Commissioners' functions were to collect information on colonial conditions, to regulate the sale of colonial land, to organize any assisted emigration based on the land revenue, to administer the Passenger Acts, and to advise the Secretary of State for the Colonies on any matters referred to them. One of the papers printed here is a set of recommendations from which the 1842 Passenger Act was drafted. After a few years, the reports settled into an established pattern, covering Australian colonies, British North America, the West Indies and Mauritius (with the coolie emigration thither from India and elsewhere), and including appendices some of which were statistical tables, others documents from the colonies or copies of laws relating to colonial affairs.

Original references

1842	[355] XXV	Passengers' Act, Com. Rep.
	(567)	Emigration, Com. Rep., appendix.
1843	(621) XXIX	Emigration, Com. Rep., appendix.
1844	(178) XXXI	Emigration, Com. Rep., appendix.
1845	[617] XXVII	Emigration, Com., 5th Rep., appendix.
1846	[706] XXIV	Emigration, Com., 6th Rep., appendix.
1847	[809] XXXIII	Emigration, Com., 7th Rep., appendix.
1847-48	[961] XXVI	Emigration, Com., 8th Rep.
	[961-II]	Emigration, Com., 8th Rep., appendix.

Emigration 11 General reports of the colonial land and emigration commissioners with appendices, 1849-52. (552 pp.)

These reports deal with emigration at a peak period. Most emigrants were Irish, and entered the United States through New York. Large sums of money were sent home, either to finance the reuniting of families or to maintain and improve relatives' standards of living. There is also much information, however, on the terms of purchase of land in British colonies, on the use of the resulting funds to finance emigration, and on problems of settling such groups as Irish female orphans in so different a society. The granting of return passages to coolies working in the West Indies is discussed.

Original references

1849	[1082] XXII	Emigration, Com., 9th Rep., appendix.
1850	[1204] XXIII	Emigration, Com., 10th Rep., appendix.
1851	[1383] XXII	Emigration, Com., 11th Rep., appendix.
1852	[1499] XVIII	Emigration, Com., 12th Rep., appendix.

Emigration 12 General reports of the colonial land and emigration commissioners with appendices, 1852-55. (664 pp.)

The commissioners provide the following information: the numbers of emigrants, their English, Scottish, Irish or foreign origin, the ports from which they sailed, their occupations, conditions on board emigrant ships and at the ports of embarkation and disembarkation, and the commissioners' own work in organizing some emigration and protecting all of it. The 1853 Report expresses relief at the decrease of Irish emigration to America and comments on the effects of emigration on the labouring population remaining in Ireland. Hundreds of pages are filled with reports of the Victoria gold rush and with regulations needed to control the influx of miners. Although most of their responsibilities continued year after year, the commissioners had to deal from time to time with new problems, such as the transporting of Chinese coolies as well as Indian.

Original references
1852-53 [1647] XL   Emigration, Com., 13th Rep., appendix.
1854   [1833] XXVIII   Emigration, Com., 14th Rep., appendix.
1854-55 [1953] XVII   Emigration, Com., 15th Rep., appendix.

Emigration 13 General reports of the colonial land and emigration commissioners with appendices, 1856-58. (616 pp.)

Prosperity in the British Isles led to a fall in emigration during the later 1850s, though the proportions going to the several overseas countries were unchanged. The commissioners note that fewer people are moving on from Canada to the United States, while many are willing to move the other way. Two matters which receive considerable attention are the social effects of immigration upon the colonies, and the need for special efforts to attain an equal balance of the sexes in Australia.

Original references
1856   [2089] XXIV   Emigration, Com., 16th Rep., appendix.
1857   [2249] XVI   Emigration, Com., 17th Rep., appendix.
Sess. 2
1857-58 [2395] XXIV   Emigration, Com., 18th. Rep., appendix.

Emigration 14 General reports of the colonial land and emigration commissioners with appendices, 1859-61. (624 pp.)

There is considerable discussion of the causes of decline in emigration, which affects Australia and New Zealand as well as America. The demand for additional troops because of the Indian Mutiny, and a commercial crisis in the United States and then in Canada, were significant; but more important was the increased prosperity of the working class, even in Ireland. The volume contains the familiar types of information about numbers of emigrants to the several colonies, conditions on board emigrant ships, land sales, problems of selecting emigrants for government assistance. New elements are the treatment of Queensland as a separate colony, and the gold rush along the Fraser River in British Columbia.

Original references

1859	[2555] XIV	Emigration, Com., 19th Rep., appendix.
Sess. 2		
1860	[2696] XXIX	Emigration, Com., 20th Rep., appendix.
1861	[2842] XXII	Emigration, Com., 21st Rep., appendix.

Emigration 15 General reports of the colonial land and emigration commissioners with appendices, 1862-64. (664 pp.)

The outbreak of the American Civil War brought about an immediate fall in British emigration; but after the first two years industrial boom and, it was alleged, prospects of enlistment in the Union army, brought figures back to a high level. At the same time there was widespread unemployment in Britain, particularly in the cotton industy. In their accounts of British colonies, the commissioners trace the effects of gold discoveries, and report on mining leases, land sales, and trade. The usual statistical information is appended. It is noteworthy that steamships are now featured prominently as a factor on the North Atlantic.

Original references

1862	[3010] XXII	Emigration, Com., 22nd Rep., appendix.
1863	[3199] XV	Emigration, Com., 23rd Rep., appendix.
1864	[3341] XVI	Emigration, Com., 24th Rep., appendix.

Emigration 16 General reports of the colonial land and emigration commissioners with appendices, 1865-66. (544 pp.)

For the most part, the reports follow the standard arrangement, whether of statistics, reports on the working of the Passenger Acts, or news of colonial assistance schemes. Steamships now carry a majority of emigrants to America. High mortality rates and some shipwrecks are reported among vessels carrying coolies, and the return of labourers to their homes is again discussed.

Original references

1865	[3526] XVIII	Emigration, Com., 25th Rep., appendix.
1866	[3679] XVII	Emigration, Com., 26th Rep., appendix.

Emigration 17 General reports of the colonial land and emigration commissioners with appendices, 1867-70. (656 pp.)

While much of the routine detail continues, the commissioners are now also concerned with cholera in North Atlantic emigrant ships, with the need to suspend coolie emigration in 1867 because of fever and commercial depression, with the types of emigrant needed in white colonies, and with the possibility of enforcing repayment for assistance given from public funds. There is a mention of Welsh emigration to Patagonia. Conditions on West Indian plantations are discussed, especially the sex ratio among Indian coolies. The 1870 report includes a statistical review of the commissioners' emigration since 1847.

Original references
1867	[3855] XIX	Emigration, Com. 27th Rep., appendix.
1867-68	[4024] XVII	Emigration, Com. 28th Rep., appendix.
1868-69	[4159] XVII	Emigration, Com. 29th Rep., appendix.
1870	[C.196] XVII	Emigration, Com. 30th Rep., appendix.

Emigration 18 General reports of the colonial land and emigration commissioners with appendices, 1871-73. (576 pp.)

The 1873 Report is distinguished by its extensive discussion of the hazards of British emigration to Latin America. Apart from this, the commissioners' final reports follow the standard pattern, though in comments and statistics alike a tendency to look back over the past three decades, and review achievements, can be seen.

Original references
1871	[C.369] XX	Emigration, Com. 31st Rep., appendix.
1872	[C.562] XVI	Emigration, Com. 32nd Rep., appendix.
1873	[C.768] XVIII	Emigration, Com. 33rd Rep., appendix.

Emigration 19 Reports, returns and correspondence relating to emigration, 1828-38. (472 pp. 4 folding maps, 1 coloured)

The 1828 report by Colonel Cockburn deals especially with opportunities for settlement in the Maritime Provinces of British North America. Later reports include two, by the commissioners of 1831-32 and by the Agent-General appointed in 1837, who were precursors of the Colonial Land and Emigration Commissioners. Among the extensive correspondence between London and the colonies there appear for the first time reports by A. C. Buchanan on arrivals of emigrant ships at Quebec. Assistance schemes for emigrants to Australian colonies are for the first time worked out.

Original references

1828	(109) XXI	Emigration, Rep.
	(148)	Emigration, Rep., appendix.
1830	(650) XXIX	Emigration from United Kingdom, return.
1831-32	(724) XXXII	Emigration, Com. Rep.
1833	(696) XXVI	Emigration from United Kingdom, return.
	(141)	Emigration, correspondence.
1834	(616) XLIV	Emigration and Crown Lands, correspondence.
1835	(87) XXXIX	Emigration, correspondence.
1836	(76) XL	Emigration, correspondence.
	(526)	Emigration, correspondence.
1837-38	(388) XL	Emigration, Agent-General Rep.
	(389)	Emigration, Canada and Australia, rep. and correspondence.

Emigration 20   Reports, returns, correspondence, and papers relating to emigration, 1839-42. (448 pp.)

Most of this volume contains correspondence between the Secretary of State and the governors of colonies, but these include many valuable enclosures, such as more of Buchanan's reports. The Australian correspondence deals with the use of land revenue to finance emigration, the prospects of expansion, and the possibility of loans to emigrants. Documents are printed concerning the appointment of T. F. Elliot, Robert Torrens and the Hon. E. E. Villiers as Colonial Land and Emigration Commissioners; and a collection of papers, which in effect makes up their first Annual Report, includes interesting evidence given before an immigration committee of the New South Wales Council.

Original references

1839	(536-I) XXXIX	Emigration, Agent-General Rep.
	(536-II)	Emigration, Agent-General Rep.
	(580)	Emigrant ships chartered by government, returns.
1840	(35) XXXIII	Land and Emigration Board, correspondence.
	(613)	Land and Emigration Board, correspondence.
1841	(436) XIII	Emigrant refugees, return.
1841	(61) III	Emigration from the United Kingdom, return.
Sess. 2		
1841	(294) XXI	Emigration of female paupers, correspondence.
1841	(60) XXVII	Emigration from Scotland, Agent-General Rep.

Emigration 21   Report, returns and correspondence relative to emigration, with appendix, 1842-43. (578 pp.)

In addition to the usual treatment of crown lands and emigration finance, and the policy for selecting emigrants to be given government aid, there is more evidence from the New South Wales immigration committee, and from a similar body in Van Diemen's Land, on the demand for labour. Papers are printed on coolie emigration both to Mauritius and the West Indies. There is a brief correspondence on the Brazilian government's immigration schemes.

Original references

1842	(231) XXXI	Emigration from the United Kingdom, return.
	(301)	Colonial Office on emigration, correspondence.
1843	(136) XXXIII	Emigrants into British West Indian colonies, return.

Emigration 22   Reports, returns and correspondence relating to emigration, 1843-53. (512 pp. 2 folding maps, 1 coloured; 2 folding diagrams, 1 coloured)

Most of the correspondence is between the Colonial Office and the Australian colonies. Land problems, expenses of government emigration vessels, depots for emigrants before embarkation, are all discussed at length, and there are numerous statistical returns. Reports of conditions on the high seas include several on individual ships.

Original references

1843	(90) XXXIV	Emigration from the United Kingdom, return.
	(323)	Emigration, governors of Australian Colonies, correspondence.
	(269)	Emigrant ship, communication.
1844	(503) XXXV	Emigrant ships, returns.
1846	(170) XLV	Emigrant ship, rep., correspondence.
1847	(255) LVI	Emigration from Ireland, return.
1847-48	(345) XLVII	Colonial Land Revenue and Emigration, return.
1849	(244) XXXVIII	Emigrant depots, Rep.
1849	(266) XLVII	Irish immigration, Liverpool, letter.
1850	(734) XL	Colonial Land and Emigration Commissioners, return.
1851	(379) XL	Board and lodging of emigrants in depots, correspondence.
	(429)	Board and lodging of emigrants in depots, correspondence.
	(243)	Board of Guardians of St. Pancras and Poor Law Board, correspondence.
	(198)	Emigrant ship, correspondence.
	(680)	Emigration from the United Kingdom, return.
1852	(245) XLIX	Number of emigrant ships leaving the United Kingdom, return.

(542)	Emigrant vessels leaving the United Kingdom, return.
1852-53 (1004) LXII	Letters received by Emigration Commissioners, return.
1852-53 (23) LXVIII	Vessels chartered by the Colonial Land and Emigration Commissioners, returns.
1852-53 (113) XCVIII	Emigrant ships and emigrants, returns.
(205)	Emigrant ships, return.

Emigration 23   Reports, returns and correspondence relating to emigration, 1854-59. (698 pp.)

The volume includes details of the establishment of Emigration Officers at all British ports, and an important set of instruction to them, from the commissioners, on the enforcement of the 1852 Passenger Act. Government emigrant ships are described in considerable detail, as is the amount of money received by the commissioners for emigration purposes. Two-thirds of the pages, however, deal with coolie emigration; and among the correspondence with colonial governors there is much on finance, discipline, and the ratio of the sexes among the labourers.

Original references

1854	(255) XLVI	Names etc. of emigration officers in the United Kingdom, return.
	(178)	Emigrant ships, Reps.
	(492)	Emigrant ships, correspondence.
1854	(300) LV	Emigration of Irish poor, returns.
1854-55	(523) XVII	Emigration from Bristol, Rep.
1856	(36) XLIV	Persons in service of Emigration Commissioners, return.
1857 Sess. 2	(238) XXVIII	Names etc. of Colonial Land and Emigration Commissioners, returns.
1859 Sess. 1	[2452] XVI	Immigration to the West India colonies, papers.
1859 Sess. 2	[288] XXII	Numbers of emigrants from the United Kingdom, return.

Emigration 24   Reports, returns, correspondence and other papers relating to emigration, 1860-71. (678 pp. 2 folding maps, 1 coloured)

In 1871 an inquiry took place into allegations of ill-treatment of coolies in British Guiana. The investigators undertook a financial review of this immigration, looked closely at the agencies through which workers were recruited in China and India, and studied colonial laws. They took evidence about the material conditions of the coolies, including wages, health and housing, and the conditions under which contracts could be renewed; and they suggested reforms. The volume also includes a historical tabulation of the commissioners' emigration to Australia and elsewhere, 1840-62; a discussion of British and foreign steamships as emigrant carriers on the North Atlantic; and a summary of colonial land laws.

Original references

1860	(350) LX	Passenger ships, returns.
1861	(342) LV	Emigration of paupers, return.
1862	(476) XXXVI	Emigrants sent out by the Emigration Board, return.
1863	(430) XXXVIII	Emigrants who left the United Kingdom, return.
	(504)	Emigrants sent out by the Emigration Board, return.
1868-69	(396) XLIII	Crown Lands and emigration, return.
1868-69	(397) L	Emigrants who left the United Kingdom, return.
1870	(179) XLIX	Emigration, colonial governors, circular.
1870	(288) LX	Passenger conveyance to America, correspondence.
1870	[C.107] LXX	Emigration to Venezuela, despatch.
	[C.155]	Emigration to Venezuela, despatch.
1871	[C.393] XX	Treatment of immigrants, British Guiana, Com. rep.
	[C.393-I]	Treatment of immigrants, Com. appendices part I.
	[C.393-II]	Treatment of immigrants, Com. appendices part II.
1871	[C.296] XLVII	Emigration, Sir Clinton Murdoch's rep.
	[C.335]	Emigration, colonial governors, correspondence.
	[C.335-I]	Emigration, colonial governors, map.
1871	[C.253] LXXII	Emigration to Venezuela, despatch.

Emigration 25   Report, returns and correspondence relating to emigration, 1872-81. (668 pp. 1 folding coloured map)

An important section of this volume deals with emigration to Brazil and the condition of British emigrants there in the form of reports sent to the Secretary of State for the colonies, Earl Granville, by officials of Her Majesty's Legation at Rio de Janeiro. The prospects of British emigrants are analysed with particular reference to intending emigrant agricultural labourers and their families. The reports contain in addition information on the experiences and circumstances of employment of immigrants in the Brazilian State colony of Cananea. Conditions and prospects for emigrants are assessed in the light of the total collapse of the Brazilian State colonization scheme. The reports refute the allegation that immigrants into the Brazilian colonies of Cananea and Assunguy have little hope of economic survival and conclude that industrious and sober immigrants can maintain themselves with a certain degree of comfort. Geographical and demographic details of these areas are supplied.

A more favourable account is given of the River Plate republics, though obstacles likely to be encountered by British emigrants are not disguised.

A Board of Trade investigation into emigrant steamships is printed. The statistical tables begin to include very detailed local figures on Ireland –

down to poor-law unions, not just counties, and with emigration to Britain identified as well as that to the colonies and the United States – together with a separate tabulation of Irish migratory labourers.

Original references

1872	[C.614] XLIII	Emigration, colonial governors, correspondence.
	(154)	Names etc. of Colonial Land and Emigration Commissioners, returns.
1872	[C.659] LXX	Argentine Confederation, Rep.
	[C.569]	British subjects in the Argentine, correspondence.
	[C.550]	Immigration to Brazil, Rep.
1873	[C.777] LXXV	Condition of British emigrants in Brazil, Reps.
1874	[C.986] LXXVI	Condition of British emigrants in Brazil, Rep.
1875	(323) LXX	*Cospatrick* emigrant ship, Rep.
1875	[C.1135] LXXXII	Emigration to Brazil, Rep.
	[C.1166]	Emigration to Brazil, Rep.
1877	(5) LXXXV	Emigration and immigration, the United Kingdom, return, Rep.
	[C.1700]	Emigration from Ireland, return.
1878	(9) LXXVII	Emigration and immigration, the United Kingdom, return, Rep.
	[C.2066]	Emigration, from Ireland, return.
1878-79	(32) LXXV	Emigration and immigration, the United Kingdom, return, Rep.
	[C.2221]	Emigration from Ireland, return.
1880	(8) LXXVI	Emigration and immigration, the United Kingdom, return, Rep.
	[C.2501]	Emigration from Ireland, return.
1881	[C.2995] LXXXII	Atlantic steamships, Rep.
1881	[C.2809] XCIII	Migratory Agricultural Irish Labourers, Rep., return.
1881	(89) XCIV	Emigration and immigration, the United Kingdom, return, Rep.
	[C.2828]	Emigration from Ireland, return.

Emigration 26   Reports, returns, correspondence and other papers relating to emigration, 1882-87. (628 pp.)

Much of the volume consists of a continuation of the several statistical series. The Medical Officers' returns provide a long list of emigrant ships, with details of each one; but this is true only of 1882 and the first half of 1883. The principal novelty, however, is the foundation of the Emigrants' Information Office in 1886.

Original references

1882	[C.3422] LV	Emigration, clauses of Arrears Act, Rep.
1882	(252) LXII	Board of Trade, return.
	(398)	Passengers and deaths on voyages, return.
	(404)	Medical officers' names, qualifications etc. return.
1882	[C.3150] LXXIV	Migratory agricultural Irish labourers, Rep., return.
	[C.3438]	Migratory agricultural Irish labourers, Rep., return.

	(87)	Emigration and immigration, the United Kingdom, return, Rep.
	[C.3170]	Emigration from Ireland, return.
1883	(261) LXII	Board of Trade, return.
1883	[C.3810] LXXVI	Migratory agricultural Irish labourers, Rep., return.
	(89)	Emigration and immigration, the United Kingdom, return, Rep.
	[C.3489]	Emigration from Ireland, return.
1884	[C.4150] LXXXV	Migratory agricultural Irish labourers, Reps.
	(9)	Emigration and immigration, the United Kingdom, return, Rep.
	[C.3899]	Emigration from Ireland, return.
1884-85	[C.4601] LXXXV	Migratory agricultural Irish labourers, Rep., return.
	(52)	Emigration and immigration, the United Kingdom, return, Rep.
	[C.4303]	Emigration from Ireland, return.
1886	[C.4751] XLV	Emigration to colonies, correspondence.
1886	[C.4806] LXXI	Migratory agricultural Irish labourers, Rep., return.
	(3)	Emigration and immigration, the United Kingdom, return, Rep.
	[C.4660]	Emigration from Ireland, return.
1887	[C.5078] LVII	Emigrants' Information Office, papers. Migratory agricultural Irish labourers, Rep., return.
1887	[C.5221] LXXXIX	Migratory agricultural Irish labourers, Rep.
	(32)	Emigration and immigration, the United Kingdom, return, Rep.
	[C.4967]	Emigration from Ireland, return.

Emigration 27   Reports, returns and correspondence relating to emigration, 1888-94. (642 pp.)

In addition to the standard statistics, the volume includes annual reports from the Emigrants' Information Office: the 1889 report has an account of a tour of Australia to examine emigration prospects. The other new feature is the series of tables on immigration into Britain, the result of the recommendations of the select committee of 1888-89.

Original references

1888	[C.5391] LXXIII	Emigrants' Information Office, Rep.
1888	[C.5403] LXXX	Colonization of Crofters, correspondence.
1888	(88) LXXXIII	Emigration from Mayo, correspondence.
1888	[C.5543] CVI	Migratory agricultural Irish labourers, Rep., return.
1888	(2) CVII	Emigration and immigration, the United Kingdom, return, Rep.
	[C.5307]	Emigration from Ireland, return.
1889	[C.5725] LV	Emigrants' Information Office, Rep.
1889	[C.5873] LXXVI	Immigration into Argentine Republic, correspondence.
1889	[C.5837] LXXXIII	Migratory Irish agricultural labourers, Rep., return.
1889	(10) LXXXIV	Emigration and immigration, the United Kingdom, return, Rep.
	[C.5647]	Emigration from Ireland, return.
1890	[C.6064] XLIX	Emigrants' Information Office, Rep.

1890	[C.6175] LXXIX	Migratory agricultural Irish labourers, Rep., return.
	(103)	Emigration and immigration, the United Kingdom, return, Rep.
	[C.6010]	Emigration from Ireland, return.
1890-91	[C.6277] LVI	Emigrants' Information Office, Rep.
1890-91	[C.6519] XCI	Migratory agricultural Irish labourers, Rep., return.
1890-91	(147) XCII	Emigration and immigration, the United Kingdom, return, Rep.
	[C.6295]	Emigration from Ireland, return.
1892	[C.6573] LVI	Emigrants' Information Office, Rep.
1892	[C.6779] LXXXVIII	Migratory agricultural Irish labourers, Rep., return.
	(134)	Emigration and immigration, the United Kingdom, return, Rep.
	[C.6679]	Emigration from Ireland, return.
1893-94	[C.6887] LX	Emigrants' Information Office, Rep.
	[C.7269]	Emigrants' Information Office, Rep.
1893-94	[C.7188] CI	Migratory agricultural Irish labourers, Rep., return.
1893-94	(138) CII	Emigration and immigration, the United Kingdom, return, Rep.
	[C.6977]	Emigration from Ireland, return.
	[C.7288]	Emigration from Ireland, return.

Emigration 28   Reports, returns and correspondence relating to emigration, 1894-99. (608 pp.)

The principal contents are again statistics of British emigration and immigration. These include the numbers, nationalities, and destinations of passengers leaving British ports, stating the numbers of adults and children, and the conjugal condition of the former. Migration to and from European ports is shown as well as movement to more distant countries. Minute local detail is provided in the tables dealing with Irish migratory labourers; and a statement of their landholdings is included, as an index to their standard of life.

Original references

1894	[C.7533] XCIII	Migratory agricultural Irish labourers, Rep., return.
1894	(90) XCIV	Emigration and immigration, the United Kingdom, return, Rep.
1895	[C.7631] LXX	Emigrants' Information Officer, Rep.
1895	(213) CVII	Emigration and immigration, the United Kingdom, return, Rep.
	[C.7647]	Emigration from Ireland, return.
1896	[C.7979] LVIII	Emigrants' Information Office, Rep.
	[C.8256]	Emigrants' Information Office, Rep., papers.
1896	[C.7957] XCII	Migratory agricultural Irish labourers, Rep., return.
	[C.8197]	Migratory agricultural Irish labourers, Rep., return.
1896	(130) XCIII	Emigration and immigration, the United Kingdom, return, Rep.
	[C.7959]	Emigration from Ireland, return.
1897	[C.8360] LXI	Emigrants' Information Office, Rep.

1897	[C.8625] XCVIII	Migratory agricultural Irish labourers, Rep., return.
1897	(165) XCIX	Emigration and immigration, the United Kingdom, return, Rep.
	[C.8366]	Emigration from Ireland, return.
1898	[C.8756] LIX	Emigrants' Information Office, Rep.
1898	[C.9006] CII	Migratory agricultural Irish labourers, Rep., return.
1898	(154) CIII	Emigration and Immigration, the United Kingdom, return, Rep.
	[C.8740]	Emigration from Ireland, return.
1899	[C.9196] LVIII	Emigrants' Information Office, Rep.
1899	[C.9490] CVI	Migratory agricultural Irish labourers, Rep., return.
1899	(188) CVII	Emigration and immigration, the United Kingdom, return, Rep.
	[C.9193]	Emigration from Ireland, return.

Bibliography

Emigration from Britain, the principal subject of our parliamentary papers, was part of a world-wide phenomenon of the nineteenth century; and it seems proper to suggest a short list of books that will help the reader place his immediate subject in perspective. Carl Wittke, *We Who Built America: the Saga of the Immigrant* (New York, 1939) deals with European migrants group by group, with primary emphasis upon their life in the United States. Marcus L. Hansen, *The Atlantic Migration 1607-1860: a History of the Continuing Settlement of the United States* (Cambridge, Mass., 1940; reprinted 1951) treats Western European migration with heavy emphasis upon background conditions. Maldwyn A. Jones, *American Immigration* (Chicago, 1960) is America-centred, and is concerned especially with the processes of assimilation. Philip Taylor, *The Distant Magnet: European Emigration to the United States* (London, 1971) also adopts a topical rather than a chronological approach, but it treats European background and the Atlantic journey more fully. It presents much evidence on work, housing and institutions in the United States, but emphasizes far less than Jones the generations after the first. There is no satisfactory overall treatment of migration within the British Empire, nor of European emigration to Latin America. Broad questions about the relationship of emigration to nineteenth-century economic developments are opened up, with the aid of abundant statistics, by Brinley Thomas, *Migration and Economic Growth* (Cambridge, 1954) and *Migration and Urban Development* (London, 1972).

The other context in which British emigration needs to be placed is the nineteenth-century system of imperial government, especially in the decades before self-government became widespread. It is enough to mention Paul Knaplund, *James Stephen and the British Colonial System 1813-1847* (Madison, Wis., 1953) and D. Murray Young, *The Colonial Office in the Early Nineteenth Century* (London, 1961), which studies internal organization and personnel from the late eighteenth century to 1830. The machinery is shown in action in H. J. M. Johnston, *British Emigration Policy 1815-1830* (Oxford, 1972) and in Peter Burroughs, *Britain and Australia 1831-1855: a Study in Imperial Relations and Crown Lands Administration* (Oxford, 1967). Both of these make better sense of their topics than any earlier studies; and the latter is a monograph of quite outstanding quality, with an exceptionally well-organized bibliography. Fred H. Hitchins, *The Colonial Land and Emigration Commission* (Philadelphia, 1931) is a solid pioneer study, which does justice to the variety of the commissioners' activities without seeking to go much beyond their own documents. For the development and working of the Passenger Acts it has been superseded by Oliver MacDonagh, *A Pattern of Government Growth: The Passenger Acts and their Enforcement 1800-60* (London, 1961). Based largely upon the Colonial Office papers, this treats the age of sail only; but it is exceedingly thorough, as well as valuable for its reflections upon connections between emigration policy and the principles of Early Victorian administration as a whole. Edward Gibbon Wakefield's ideas are fully set forth in his *England and America* 2 vols. (London, 1833; reprinted by Augustus Kelley, Clifton, N.J.); and the

Collected Works, ed. M. F. Lloyd Pritchard (London, 1968) also contains this key publication. There is a lengthy summary in Richard C. Mills, *The Colonization of Australia 1829-42: The Wakefield Experiment in Empire-Building* (London, 1915) and a modern discussion, running through several chapters, in Donald Winch, *Classical Political Economy and Colonies* (London, 1965). The standard view in Charles P. Lucas, *The Durham Report* 3 vols. (Oxford, 1912) is challenged by Ged Martin, *The Durham Report and British Policy: a Critical Essay* (Cambridge, 1972) but no concern is shown for emigration matters.

The facts of British emigration, and some aspects of policy too, are set forth in two early books which are still often cited. Stanley C. Johnson, *A History of Emigration from the United Kingdom to North America 1763-1912* (London, 1913) is arranged topically. William A. Carrothers, *Emigration from the British Isles* (London, 1929) leans equally upon parliamentary papers and is equally unrealistic in its emphasis on assistance schemes, but is more chronological and deals with colonies other than the North American. Although both have statistical tables, the fullest source of figures is now N. M. Carrier and J. R. Jeffery, *External Migration: A Study of the Available Statistics 1815-1950* (London, 1953).

Treating British emigration to the United States are two books by Wilbur S. Shepperson, *British Emigration to North America: Projects and Opinions in the Early Victorian Period* (Oxford, 1957) and *Emigration and Disenchantment: Portraits of Englishmen Repatriated from the United States* (Norman, Okla., 1965). It should be observed that very few of the projects had any practical effect. Long essays in *Perspectives in American History*, VII (1973) treat British emigration to the United States (Maldwyn A. Jones), background conditions in the Scottish Lowlands (Malcolm Gray), and Welsh emigration (Alan Conway). Charlotte Erickson, *Invisible Immigrants: the Adaptation of English and Scottish Immigrants in Nineteenth-Century America* (London, 1972) is based on letters never designed for publication and therefore devoid of propaganda purpose. It classifies the writers by occupations within the United States; and the lengthy commentaries are firmly grounded in censuses, county histories, and the like, as well as in the letters themselves, so that backgrounds in Britain as well as fortunes in America can be traced. Dr. Erickson deals briefly with a wider problem in her contribution 'Who were the English and Scots Emigrants to the United States in the late Nineteenth Century?' in D. V. Glass and Roger Revelle, *Population and Social Change* (London, 1972). Rowland T. Berthoff, *British Immigrants in Industrial America* (Cambridge, Mass., 1952) deals first with immigrants in one industry after another, then with aspects of their adjustment to American society or their resistance to it. Closely related is Charlotte Erickson, *American Industry and the European Immigrant 1860-1885* (Cambridge, Mass., 1957), though her immigrants are far from exclusively British. Alan Conway, *The Welsh in America* (Cardiff, 1961) has interesting letters, about the background and journey as well as experiences in the United States.

On Irish emigration, there is less of high quality than might be expected. R. J. Dickson, *Ulster Emigration to Colonial America 1718-1775* (London, 1966) and Maldwyn A. Jones, 'Ulster Emigration 1783-1815' in *Essays in Scotch-Irish History*, ed. E. R. Green (London,

1969) may be followed by William F. Adams, *Ireland and Irish Emigration to the New World from 1815 to the Famine* (New Haven, Conn., 1932). Oliver MacDonagh has a chapter on emigration, packed with detail, in *The Great Famine*, ed. R. Dudley Edwards and T. Desmond Williams (Dublin, 1956). The later years of the century are treated rather sketchily in Arnold Schrier, *Ireland and the American Emigration 1850-1900* (Minneapolis, 1958). Four articles by the geographer S. H. Cousens are also of great interest: 'The Regional Variations in Emigration from Ireland between 1821 and 1841', *Transactions of the Institute of British Geographers*, XXXVII (1965), pp. 15-29; in the same journal, XXVIII (1960), pp. 119-34, 'The Regional Pattern of Emigration during the Great Famine 1846-51'; 'Emigration and Demographic Change in Ireland 1851-1861', *Economic History Review*, Second Series, XIV (1961), pp. 275-88; and in the same journal, XVII (1964), pp. 301-21, 'The Regional Variations in Population Change in Ireland 1861-1881'.

For the North Atlantic crossing, see especially Terry Coleman, *Passage to America* (London, 1972). The emigrants he treats are mainly Irish. For a briefer treatment of a wider period see P. Taylor, *The Distant Magnet*, chapter 7, while chapter 8 deals with the steamship years. Because most books focus on the higher classes of passengers, or on the ships for their own sake, it is useful to consult two primary sources on steamship crossings: Robert Louis Stevenson, *The Amateur Emigrant* (1879) in *Works*, XVIII. Tusitala Edition. 35 vols. (London, 1924) and 'An Emigrant's Letter from Iowa 1871', ed. Charlotte Erickson, *Bulletin* of the British Association for American Studies, New Series, XII and XIII (1966), pp. 11-16.

Dealing with British North America, before Confederation, is Helen I. Cowan, *British Emigration to British North America: the First Hundred Years* (Toronto, 1928, Rev. ed. 1961). Norman MacDonald, *Canada 1763-1841, Immigration and Settlement: the Administration of the Imperial Land Regulations* (London, 1939) has a different emphasis, as the sub-title indicates; and his theme is taken into even greater detail in Lillian F. Gates, *Land Policies of Upper Canada* (Toronto, 1968) and Alan Wilson, *The Clergy Reserves of Upper Canada: a Canadian Mortmain* (Toronto, 1968). Macdonald's second monograph, *Canada: Immigration and Colonization 1841-1903* (Aberdeen, 1966) is wider in scope and based on careful research; but it makes heavy reading and its documentation is extremely hard to follow. Two studies treat the important but difficult question of how many Canadian immigrants crossed the border into the United States, and how many Americans, of whatever origin, moved north: Marcus L. Hansen, *The Mingling of the Canadian and American Peoples* (New Haven, Conn., 1940) and Leon C. Truesdell, *The Canadian-born in the United States* (New Haven, Conn., 1943).

On Australia, the pioneer work is R. C. Mills, *The Colonization of Australia* (London, 1915) though most scholars would now agree that he makes Wakefield's ideas seem even more important than they were. Stephen H. Roberts, *History of Australian Land Settlement, 1788-1920* (Melbourne, 1924) covers so much ground that some chapters seem not much more than summaries of enactments, and the maps are too small for their purpose; but especially for the decades after 1850 there is no substitute. The same writer's *The Squatting Age in Australia, 1835-1847*

(Melbourne, 1935; reprinted: 1965) is far more interesting to read, whether on daily life or policy-making; but some details have been challenged by Burroughs and others. Both Roberts' books have full bibliographies of local primary sources. Aspects of single colonies are dealt with in James S. Battye, *Western Australia: a History from its Discovery to the Inauguration of the Commonwealth* (Oxford, 1924); A. Grenfell Price, *The Foundation and Settlement of South Australia* Adelaide, 1924) and Ronald M. Hartwell, *The Economic Development of Van Diemen's Land, 1820-1850* (Melbourne, 1954), which is exhaustive on balance-of-payments questions as well as internal conditions, and which has an excellent bibliography. A. G. L. Shaw, *Convicts and Colonies* (London, 1966) is an admirable study, giving due attention to the British background of transportation as well as to colonial practice. A special study of the British origins of a small number of emigrants is Ross Duncan, 'Case Studies in Emigration: Cornwall, Gloucestershire and New South Wales 1875-1886', *Economic History Review,* Second Series, XVI pp. 272-89.

On other colonial areas, there are only a few monographs of value to report. For New Zealand, see Johannes S. Marais, *The Colonization of New Zealand* (London, 1927) which deals with the first two decades. For Natal, see Alan F. Hattersley, *The British Settlement of Natal* (Cambridge, 1950). There is nothing of comparable quality on emigration to the Cape Colony.

On coolie emigration, the leading authority is now Hugh Tinker, *A New System of Slavery: the export of Indian labour overseas 1830-1920* (London, 1974). I. M. Cumpston, *Indians Overseas in British Territories 1834-1854* (London, 1953), is a good pioneer study of a short period. The other major group is rather thinly treated, for Canada, Australia and Malaya as well as the West Indies, in Persia C. Campbell, *Chinese Coolie Emigration to Countries within the British Empire* (London, 1923, reprinted New York, 1969). A single colony is the subject of two recent studies, Michael Moohr, 'The Economic Impact of Slave Emancipation in British Guiana 1832-1852', *Economic History Review,* Second Series, XXV (1972), pp. 588-607; Alan H. Adamson, *Sugar Without Slaves: the Political Economy of British Guiana 1838-1904* (New Haven, Conn., 1972).

On immigration into Britain in the nineteenth century, it is sufficient to note the following: James E. Handley, *The Irish in Scotland, 1798-1845* (Cork, 1943) and *The Irish in Modern Scotland* (Cork, 1947); Lloyd P. Gartner, *The Jewish Immigrant in England, 1870-1914* (London, 1960); John A. Garrard, *The English and Immigration: a Comparative Study of the Jewish Influx, 1880-1910* (London, 1971). Gartner is concerned with social conditions, Garrard mainly with attitudes and policies.

[Items late for inclusion in the body of the bibliography: Brinley Thomas, *Migration and Economic Growth,* 2nd ed. (1973); Hugh Tinker, *A New System of Slavery: the export of Indian labour overseas 1830-1920* (London, 1974).]

It will be clear from this bibliography that the weakness in our stock of monographs lies in the second half of the nineteenth century. My argument in the Commentary suggests that research output has reflected the supply of parliamentary papers and the manuscripts that lie behind them.

Index

All references are to page numbers. The prefix 'n' indicates a reference to a footnote on the page cited.

T